The Seven Steps to Sanity

How to Balance Work & Play

Jennifer Jefferies ND

THE SEVEN STEPS TO SANITY – HOW TO BALANCE WORK & PLAY
Copyright Jennifer Jefferies 2002
First published in Australia 2002
Second Edition 2003

Published By
Living Energy Natural Therapies
Website: www.livingenergy.com.au
Email: jennifer@livingenergy.com.au

National Library of Australia cataloguing – in-publication data
    Jefferies, Jennifer Lee
        Seven Steps to Sanity

    ISBN 0 9578181 1 4.

    1. Title. 1. Aromatherapy 2. Health

DISCLAIMER

The information contained in this book is not intended as medical advice, but as general information only. The author/publisher cannot accept responsibility for any mishap resulting from the use of essential oils, or other therapeutic methods described in this book. My advice to the reader is to realise you are an individual, and as such, I recommend you consult a professional Aromatherapist or health care professional if treatment or advice is required.

Typesetting by Living Energy, Townsville.
Printed by Watson & Ferguson, Brisbane

Dedication

To my life partner Ms Toni Esser for cruizing the
highways of life with me.

Thank you also for being a balanced and guiding light
in my life.

Thank you also to my parents
who have taught me so much about life in the past year,
through their own experiences in finding that balance and
renewed passion for life in their retirement.

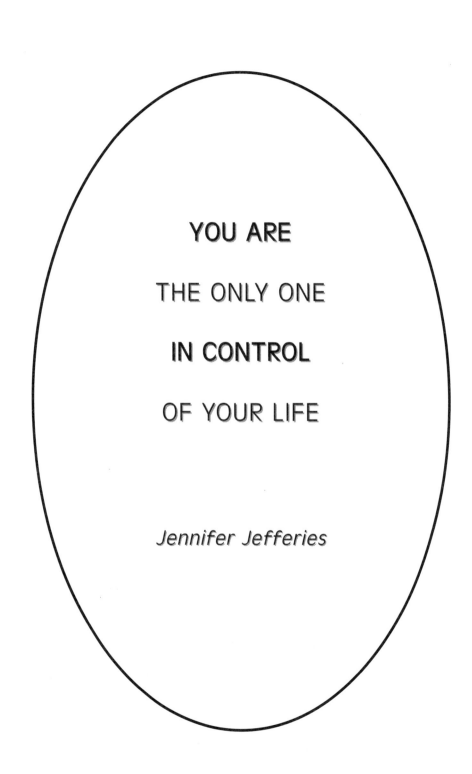

YOU ARE

THE ONLY ONE

IN CONTROL

OF YOUR LIFE

Jennifer Jefferies

Contents

Chapter

The Seven Steps to Sanity

1. Respect Yourself, Say NO!
2. Live with Balanced Nutrition.
3. Live with Realistic Fitness Levels
4. Have FUN
5. Maintain one calendar.
6. Live your dreams NOW.
7. Remember – You're Human.
   "The world won't end"

Chapter 1

Respect Yourself, Say NO!

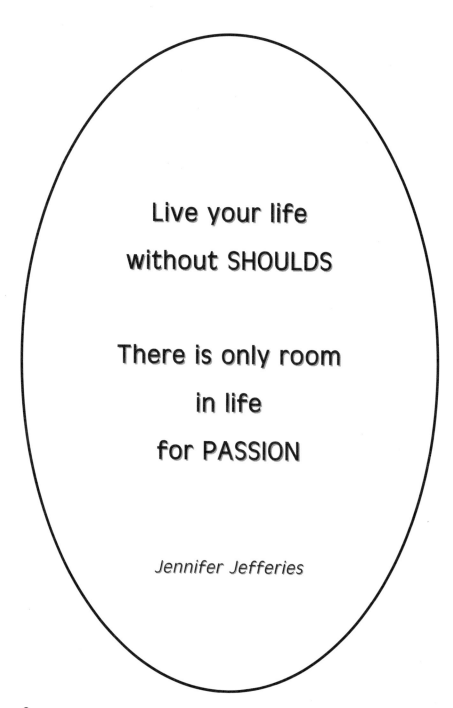

Live your life

without SHOULDS

There is only room

in life

for PASSION

Jennifer Jefferies

We all know that we are our own worst enemies when it comes to saying yes to every request that is asked of us. In my clinic over the years I have found that it seems to be bred into women in particular that we have to say yes to every request that is made of us. And if we say *NO!*, we are being selfish and not caring for the person who made the request of us in the first place.

Well I think different, I think it is time for us to show some respect to ourselves and start saying *NO!* It does not mean that we do not care or we are being selfish. It simply means that we understand that if we take on that additional task we may not be able to perform it and other previously committed tasks properly. So why not say *NO!* to the new request and be able to perform at our best on all levels.

You may shock the person requesting at first but they will understand that you are treating yourself with a different sense of self-respect and they will appreciate it in the long run. If they cannot get their heads around it, you saying no has pushed their buttons for a reason.

Now you have to use tact and speak from your heart when you say *NO!* especially in a work situation. If you speak from your heart you speak your truth and you will not just come across as a cold hearted person who is saying *NO!*. Maybe part of the transition process is saying *NO!* in steps.

I remember when I first was placed into a management position, I was told that if I had something to delegate, give it to a busy person because they would get it done. Well that worked for me but what about the poor person I was loading up. It wasn't long before they felt teh stress and also started saying *NO!* I realised that when they started saying *NO!* as well, I had to look at other solutions.

What we did was design a system to complete work in a way that everyone felt comfortable. It may have been delegating tasks further down the chain or setting up a system where tasks were handled by a regular person and did not keep coming up as a priority. The end result was that everyone became less burdened and the team functioned more efficiently. People were no longer being placed into the uncomfortable position of saying *NO!* The system was used to rectify the problem. It is not usually the person that is causing the unbalanced result; it is the lack of a system in the first place. We have always told our team that they are allowed to think outside of the box. If they make mistakes, it is okay because it means we simply have to write a system to support them in their work. This does not mean that you lose control of your business and bend down to your team. It means that you are fixing the problem in advance so that everyone involved can stay balanced.

Authors Thorwald Dethlefsen and Rudiger Dahlke of The Healing Power of Illness write:

"Illness is a human condition which indicates that the patient is no longer in order or in harmony at the level of consciousness. The

loss of inner balance manifests itself in the body as a symptom. The symptom is at one and the same time a signal and a vehicle for information, for its appearance interrupts our life's familiar flow and forces us to give the symptom our attention"

Now days my partner Toni and I work from our office at home, and we have designed basic systems so that we both understand our responsibilities and tasks. This way we do not have to worry about the saying *NO!* When it comes to speaking clients, again our system is set, if the work being requested by the client fits our criteria and is going to take our business in the direction we desire, we take the booking. If it does not we comfortably and respectfully say *NO!* and refer the person onto someone who can help them.

Saying *NO!* and staying balanced, comes the responsibility of listening to your self-talk, I also found that people were setting themselves up for extra challenges in life just by the way they were speaking.

We have a rule within our work and home environments, that we do not use negative words, and especially, double negatives. My pet hates are " no worries", "no problem", "no hassles" etc. When you ask someone for something and they say "no worries", their body actually hears the negative worry part. No and worries for instance, are two very negative words tied together.

We already have enough stress in the world and any edges that we can trim will help. Through my personal experience, using positives like "it's easy" as a substitute, works. These are not the only ones, but just listen to yourself. Notice how many negative words you use and how many times you use them. It is simply a habit that we have learned and it can be corrected very easily, if the desire is there.

Some people may think, "How important is that?" When Toni and I first replaced "no worries" with "it's easy", reactions were visible on people's faces. The effects were instantly noticeable, and it set us apart as being positive and different from our business competitors and others.

"It's easy" is a positive response so simple and basic. It is almost ridiculous. But our bodies hear what we say out loud and inwardly. Imagine if everything in your personal and business life was easy! What a pleasure work and life could be, and they *can* be, if you choose. Try it and enjoy people's reactions.

YOUR SELF-TALK

We have all heard of how keeping a positive mental attitude helps to keep us balanced. Using positive self-talk, or keeping a positive mental attitude, is invaluable. Our self talk is that little voice that tells us from time to time that we are *"not good enough"*, *"it's too hard"*, or that we *"cannot do"* something. We are in control of our self-talk, and yet so many people let it control them. Those little messages we give ourselves can create negative or positive belief systems, or attitudes, about ourselves. This is the root of so many major ailments, and we literally feed it with our negative self-talk.

Anyone and everyone can be positive and in control of their self-talk and their lives, if the desire is there. So, if you are sick of feeling out of control, and down in the dumps, negative and depressed, deciding to do something about it is the biggest part of the journey.

But as previously mentioned, be aware of what you say and do, catching yourself off guard when you use negative self talk. Give yourself a pat on the back and be happy when you do catch yourself out. Your old pattern was *not* noticing and *not* correcting it. If you punish yourself with more negative self-talk, you simply reinforce the negative. Instead, reinforce the positive and be happy that at least you noticed. It may be happening frequently at first, but that is OK. We are all individuals and we will handle things differently.

LEVERAGE YOUR TIME

I heard Brad Sugars mention this at one of his workshops. Think of your hourly rate, and now add on a zero. This is now your new hourly rate. You now have permission to not do anything in life that costs you less than your hourly rate. Think about it, what can you really do with your time if you outsource or eliminate the menial tasks in life. Pay someone to do the menial tasks of life such as ironing, cleaning, mowing the lawn etc… and maximize your time in more productive and life balanced projects.

Dr John Harrison, author of "Love Your Disease" illustrated the reason people get ill very well when he said *"People get ill to get what they want (caring, etcetera)" and "People do not get what they want (caring, etcetera) so they become ill."*

"Let your inspiration feed others, and give them the juice to grow, and to glow."

- Sark

Chapter 2

Live with Balanced Nutrition

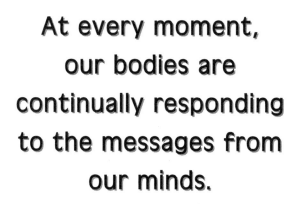

At every moment,
our bodies are
continually responding
to the messages from
our minds.

So what messages is your mind
giving your body?

Margo Adair

As a naturopath I work with peoples nutritional status all of the time. Like the general population I was raised by nutritional information of the time. That was the classic Food Pyramid, with the major food group to be consumed being grains. It is interesting that when graziers want to fatten up cattle, they feed them grains. Over the past twenty years we have seen an explosion in the incidence of obesity in the western world. People are consuming grains and in most cases refined grains in excess to what their bodies require. All of the adverts on the television saying to eat different breakfast cereals, because they are "Iron man foods", are misleading. They are Iron man foods for people doing the quantity of exercise that an Iron man does. If a child has a healthy serving of cereal and then sits their behind all day at school, they are not going to burn up the excess calories contained within. The result is an increase in body fat. Now as I have said throughout this book, grains and carbs are okay provided that they are unrefined and that they are consumed in balance with the other food groups.

The food pyramid that I use as a naturopath differs to the one generally used by dieticians. The diagram on the next page details what I recommend.

FOOD PYRAMID

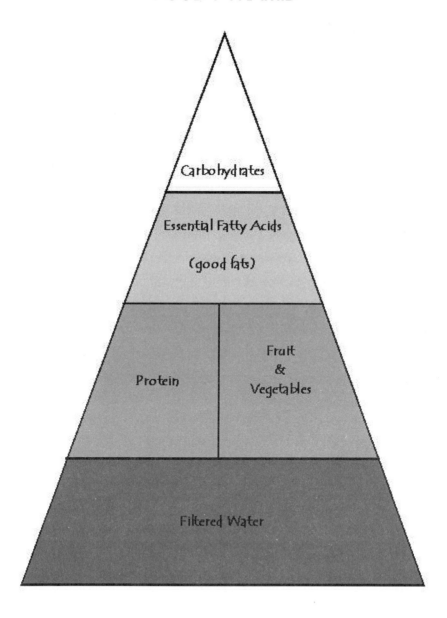

Lets consider the food groups of my food pyramid.

FILTERED PURE WATER

At the bottom of the pyramid is water. Water is critical to fundamental cell chemistry. By weight we need more of it than any other dietary substance, as it provides multiple detoxification benefits and removes acidic waste released during athletic activity. That's why its purity is such an important issue. As suggested throughout this book I recommend consuming 2-4 liters of filtered water per day, which is how much an active person needs just to prevent dehydration. This means you're consuming on average a thousand litres per year. That's a lot of water, potentially contaminated with chlorine, bacteria, parasites, heavy metals and literally thousands of toxic industrial chemicals.

Whether you use distilled water, water filtered by carbon and reverse osmosis, or some of the newer "living" bottled waters does not concern me. Just ensure that the water has been through a filtering system of some kind and that you consume your quota daily.

FRESH ORGANIC FRUITS & VEGETABLES

Vegetables are typically high in carbohydrates and rich sources of potassium and magnesium, which makes them alkaline-forming. Vegetables supply us with an excellent source of pure water, enzymes, carotenoids, fibre & antioxidants. Eat at least 3-5 times more vegetables per day than fruit. Raw vegetables provide hidden antioxidant value behind every color and pigment.

The general rule with fruit is to consume them before noon or after exercise when insulin sensitivity is highest. Like vegetables, fruits consist mainly of carbohydrates but in a more concentrated, simple sugar (high GI) form. They are good sources of some rather exotic but powerful antioxidants, which improve capillary strength and strengthen the immune system by scavenging free radicals.

Juicing is beneficial, the difference between freshly squeezed juice and the canned, bottled or boxed variety is that fresh juice is alive, alkaline forming and teeming with enzymes, whereas virtually all commercial juices are deactivated, acid forming and "dead" as a result of being pasteurized. Vitamin C and the bioflavonoids are destroyed by heat.

Bottled and canned juices are frequently loaded with sucrose, fructose, artificial colors & flavors and a host of other chemicals, most of which are not listed on the label. One such offender is brominated oil (BO), added to prevent settling and the formation of "rings". BO is known to cause changes in heart tissue, enlarge the thyroid gland and cause problems with the liver. Take the time to freshly squeeze your own.

Remember it is important to eat the fruit or vegetable whole majority of the time, so that you get the fibre as well. If you are making your own juice put some of the pulp back into the juice and then drink it. By using the pulp as well, you lower the glycemic index of the drink.

 ## QUALITY PROTEIN

Dead Animal (Meats) - If you want to eat meats, that is your decision, I only ask that you eat good quality meats. Commercial, domesticated meats are typically high in saturated fat (sirloin steak is 72% fat) and provide little or no essential omega-3 fatty acids. Farmed meats are frequently contaminated with pesticides, antibiotics, parasites, prions, salmonella and E. coli. Processed meats are just scary, with next to no nutritional value, the overheating used in processing meats creates rancid/mutagenic products that have no place in a persons diet. Go for organic meats, free from too much of mans intervention. Our local butcher was telling us that he considers lamb to be the best meat, because they are killed so young; they have spent their lives playing in the paddock with little intervention. Pretty sad, but true. Whatever you decide, go for quality and not quantity. If you are on a budget, you are better off having an organic steak weekly than having low quality sausages or mince daily. Also remember to trim any excess fat (white bits) off the meat before cooking.

Egg Whites and egg substitutes - My personal preference for quality protein, is egg whites. They are loaded with protein, very low in calories and have no cholseterol. My favourite breakfasts are an egg white omlette or the absolute favourite is pan cakes. For pan cakes use the following recipe:

Beat raw rolled oats into 2 egg whites and cook in a hot pan (no oil) , top with low fat cottage cheese, fruit and a little real maple syrup.

The egg whites mixed with the oats is fantastic for after a morning training. This recipe comes from Pam Brown, Pam is a woman who trasnformed her body through the "Body for Life" program.

Always cook your egg whites fully as there can be a risk of salmonella poisoning with raw egg. It is handy to have some ready boiled eggs in the refrigerator for a quick snack or to add to a meal. The humble egg is a superior source of quality protein.

Cultured Low-Fat Dairy Products - When consumed direct from the breast, human milk is raw, suited biologically for our species and teeming with important friendly bacteria, colostrum, enzymes,

HMB, GLA, DHA and other fatty acids not present in infant formula. On the other hand, commercial cow's milk is pasteurized, homogenized, reinforced with synthetic additives and typically contains residue's of hormones, antibiotics and pesticides derived from grains fed to cattle.

If you want to get lean stop drinking milk. There are many sources of milk on the market today, including rice milk and soy milk. Read the packets carefully, the majority of the rice milks in the supermarket contain loads of added sugar and soy milks are taken from genetically modified (GM) soy beans. Educate yourself, read the labels. If you want to have milk, go for low fat soy (not GM) and if you prefer rice milk look for no added sugar.

In my experience the prefered dairy protein comes from soured, plain "active-culture" milk products like *low fat* yogurt, cottage cheese, kefir and feta cheese. They are much easier to digest and will provide the balance of protein, carbohydrate and fat.

Lentils, Legumes, Nuts & Seeds - Another wonderful source of protein are legumes and lentils. Vegetarians have thrived for years without intaking animal products. Again go for quality. Nuts and seeds are high in fat (68-78%) good fat, but in excess it is still fat. They are a solid source of protein, minerals and fat-soluble nutrients. The good oils found in nuts and seeds are easily damaged by heat, light and oxygen, as their oils are volatile and therefore prone to rancidity. Always purchase unsalted nuts and seeds, still in their shells. Lentils and legumes are also a source of low GI carbohydrate.

 # ESSENTIAL FATTY ACIDS

The Good Oils - The primary purpose of consuming fat is to obtain the two essential fatty acids, linoleic acid (omega-6) and alpha-linolenic acid (omega-3). Fatty acids are a critical structural component of our brain, nervous system and cell membranes. Without them and especially omega-3, we are destined to experience chronic inflammation, water retention (edema) and loss of tissue elasticity. Good fats also transport fat-soluble vitamins A, D, E & K, alpha-lipoic acid, GLA, EPA, DHA, the carotenoids, various phytosterols and the phospholipids (lecithin) around the body. We need fats in our diet, we just have to ensure that they are the good fats and are still consumed in moderation.

One of the best books I have ever read is *"Fats That Heal, Fats That Kill"*, by Udo Erasmus. He explains in basic terms the nutritional differences in lifeless, refined and processed oils compared to cold pressed oils full of nutrients. The majority of oils in the supermarket have been heated excessively in the processing and are now rancid. Margarines are even worse. Focus on eating your foods as close to nature as possible, ie cold pressed oils, rich in what your body needs to keep it functioning at its best. Personally I take organic flax or hemp seed and extra virgin olive oils daily in my diet. I add them to salads or protein shakes to give me my necessary quota of essential fatty acids. Other food sources of good fats are avocado and cold water fish. Try to avoid tinned fish as it has been exposed to extreme heats during the cooking process, this makes the good fats, not so good. Fresh is best, even the supermarkets in our local area sell fresh salmon and tuna in their deli. So if it is available in regional areas, it is even more available in the cities. There are no excuses for anyone to cheat and buy canned foods.

CARBOHYDRATES

Whole Grains - Cereal grains are high in carbohydrates. If you are going to eat grains, the germ i.e. wheat germ, should never be removed, as the germ is where the majority of nutrients live. Refined and processed grains are acid-forming (high in phosphorous) and when consumed as flour, tend to cause problems in the gut like bloating, the brain and in joint capsules. If you want to have grains in your diet, balance them with protein and fruit and vegetables in every meal. Always ensure that you consume brown grains, i.e brown rice, pasta and breads. Anything that is made with refined white wheat can be made on stone ground whole meal,rice flour or rye flour. Time to change the family over to foods that give them energy instead of draining the life out of them.

Natural Sweeteners – If you want something sweet, stick to raw honey, crude molasses and real maple syrup, in balance and moderation they are fine to add to a diet. Avoid empty calorie, granulated white sugars, refined sucrose, fructose, corn syrup and glucose-fructose. Refined sugars are addictive, immunosuppressive and will destroy your body's ability to regulate blood sugar and insulin metabolism. Levels in excess of 5 kilograms of sucrose per year accelerates aging, creates a breeding ground for yeast and fungus in the GI tract and will leach important minerals from vital organ reserves.

The average person consumes in excess of 50 kilos of sugar per year. Sugars are hidden in everything, packaged, processed foods are dangerous, as in most cases you are not even aware of what you are really eating. Get them out of your diet.

Life is like a mirror, if one area of your life (like your health) is out of balance, it reflects in all areas (such as your business and personal lives). The way you feel about yourself and life can very much be influenced by your nutritional health. The following are a few of the basic nutrients which I find people regularly deficient in. These deficiencies have the following negative affects in the physical and emotional performance of your body in day-to-day life.

CHROMIUM
Obesity, Moods, Emotions and Heart Disease

Chromium is an essential trace element, which is essential for the metabolism of insulin in the body. It is this function that gives chromium the edge in being able to handle glucose and prevent hypoglycaemia (too much insulin) and diabetes (not enough insulin). Chromium helps to regulate blood sugar levels.

Have you ever noticed when you have a big feed at lunch time that you are ready for a sleep one hour later. Depending on the levels of chromium in your body, your blood sugar can be running the roller coaster and your body's moods, emotions and energy levels will ride the roller coaster with it.

The dramatic fluctuations in energy levels and moods is referred to as a person being hypoglycaemic. Our bodies are designed to be fed regularly, before our blood sugar levels drop too low. If you are having the standard three meals a day without healthy snacks, there is a high chance you are playing with your blood sugar levels. Apart from low chromium levels leading to hypoglycaemia over time, you can also be setting yourself up for an increased chance of experiencing obesity, diabetes and or heart disease.

The incidence of Type 2 Diabetes, Obesity and Cardiovascular disease is on the increase in our country. An underlying chromium deficiency maybe contributing to and or exacerbating these conditions. Over the years in my clinic the majority of patients I saw were overworked small business people. These people were burning the candle at both ends and eating the standard three meals per day and the majority had a chromium deficiency.

A body, which is not utilising insulin effectively, can see an increased risk of cardiovascular disease, obesity, hypoglycemia, diabetes, hypertension and elevated cholesterol. Recent studies have shown Chromium supplementation to decrease total cholesterol by 7% and decrease LDL (the bad cholesterol) by 10.5% in six weeks.

Chromium can also be an integral part of any weight control program, as we all know calorie restriction is not successful for treating obesity, where supplementation with chromium can contribute to long term success. Insulin potentates the entry of glucose and amino acids into muscle cells and insulin resistance or insulin deficiency accelerates the development of obesity. In exercising, chromium increases muscle bulk and lean body mass, while decreasing body fat, giving an overall effect of a leaner and firmer physique. Which is what most of us desire.

Chromium also plays a part in diabetes. In Type 2 Diabetes, there may be normal levels or, usually an over production of insulin. The problem arises when the body becomes resistant to its effects. In western developed countries, impaired insulin sensitivity is present in about 25% of non-diabetic adults. Over 80% of type 2 diabetics respond positively to daily Chromium supplementation.

Chromium deficiency can also cause elevated cholesterol levels and aortic plaques (toxic build up in arteries of the heart). Blood Chromium levels are considerably lower in patients with coronary artery disease than others.

Foods rich in Chromium

- honey
- brown grains
- grapes
- raisins
- brewers yeast
- corn oil
- mushrooms

It is the refined and processed foods, void of chromium and other minerals that have led us to these deficiencies in the first place. Once a food has been refined it can become like a leech. The remaining constituents of the food bind onto any useful minerals in the meal and drain them out through the usual eliminating body systems.

There are several forms of Chromium available in supplements. Chromium found in brewers yeast is highly bio-available but not suitable for many people. Yeast free chromium and Chromium picolinate are also available and usable by all. More than half of all patients with glucose intolerance and adult onset diabetes become well again with chromium supplementation.

Using Chromium picolinate, *Raymond Press at Mercy Hospital in San Diego has shown that some long term insulin dependant diabetics can reduce their need for insulin.(3)* Dosage will differ from person to person depending on the condition of their body. Contact your local Naturopath for further advice.

MAGNESIUM AND STRESS

Nowdays people experience the most incredible ranges of emotions, ranging from grief and fear to realisation that we have to get on with our lives through this time of uncertainty. During these times it is even more important to remember to focus on our physical and emotional health and the interaction between the two, so that we can emotionally handle what may lie ahead.

Magnesium is a simple mineral that is needed for you to handle the emotional and physical stresses of life. For those of you who have been experiencing the pressures of life lately, the following are some of the symptoms of magnesium deficiency you may identify with: anxiety, hyper-irritability, disturbed sleep, muscle cramps, increased perspiration and or body odour, over sensitivity to heat, light and noise, urinary frequency, constipation and craving salty foods.

Common causes of magnesium deficiency are increased excretion from emotional and or physical stress. Foods high in phytates like refined grains and cereals (i.e. white bread) interfere with magnesium absorption, causing the minerals to be excreted instead of being used. Alcohol and magnesium also do not mix, and when some people stress, they drink alcohol. This only exacerbates the problem. For those of you stress bunnies that are also adrenal junkies, when either the medullary or cortical portions of the adrenals work overtime, they also trigger the excretion of magnesium. An increase in the intake of magnesium rich foods and supplements will help to reduce this over activity and allow you to relax. Medications like diuretics and laxatives can also interfere with magnesium absorption.

Foods rich in Magnesium:

- dark green vegetables
- brown grains
- brown cereals
- almonds
- pecans
- walnuts
- sunflower seeds

Including these in your diet on a daily basis and removing the draining elements like white bread, you can prevent the impact of some of life's events on your health.

Take some time to make some simple changes to your diet or talk to your naturopath about a supplement or dietary advice. Magnesium comes in tablet and powder form, both are pleasant and easy to take.

BASIC NUTRITION AND BODY FAT

There is a difference between a skinny body with a low percentage lean muscle mass and a high body fat percentage and a well proportioned body that has low body fat percentage and a high percentage lean muscle. Just start to notice what people really look like. Have a real look at people's arms, it is a good starting point, super models are a good example. They are skinny but you can see they have no muscle tone or shape to them; they can and regularly have a higher body fat percentage than someone a larger size that has muscle tone and form.

The ideal is the balance, where you are lean enough to have basic muscle definition and are not carrying any excess body fat for your size and age. Your local gym can do a body composition analysis to determine your body fat percentages. You might be surprised at what your levels are.

So how do you drop your body fat percentage and increase you lean body mass percentage. The bottom line is either reduce the energy (calories) you intake per day or increase the amount of energy (calories) you use or burn up per day. You would have the muscle there, it is just that it hides beneath that layer of fat we all store at different times of our lives.

Caloric restriction is not always successful in treating obesity, the same as doing lots of cardiovascular exercise (jogging/walking etc) isn't. Diets and cardio exercise are notoriously ineffective in long term weight reduction with long term studies showing most people regain their lost weight. If you concentrate on dropping calories and doing cardio, you will eventually lose weight but stay the same shape. If you balance calories, increase cardio and resistance exercise (basic weights) you will lose weight and transform your body shape by turning into a fat burning machine.

One recent study published in the *Journal of Applied Physiology* shows that when it comes to burning fat, weight training cannot be beaten. Thirty active men were randomly placed in one of three groups. The first ran or jogged, the second worked out with weights and the third combined both in a cross training program.

Fitness analyses taken after the subjects exercised three days per week for ten weeks showed that weight lifters increased their base metabolic rate by more than 6 percent, while cross trainers increased their metabolic rates by 4.6 percent. The group than ran or jogged didn't experience any improvements in metabolic rate. Time to include weight training into your program.

THE BALANCED DIET

Six meals a day

If you are looking for a basic recipe for a balanced diet, an easy way is to go for 6 aeroplane sized meals per day. You know the size meal they feed you on an aeroplane. Only you are going for a higher nutritiously balanced meal. An easy way to measure is to look at the size of your palm of your hand. You need one palm-sized portion of protein, carbohydrate and fruits or vegetables with each meal. And it is not what you do 5% of the time that counts; it is what you do 95% of the time that matters.

So many people ask me how to remember what is a protein or a carbohydrate. It is easy! If it comes from an animal product or legume it is protein i.e. red and white meats, fish, dairy, soy products etc. If it comes out of the ground it is a carbohydrate i.e. whole grains like bread, rice, pasta, potatoes etc. And the rest of the wholefoods are your fruits and vegetables. So aim for a balanced portion of each at each meal and you will notice the difference. Just remember you are not eating 6 large meals per day, they are six small meals. The end result is that you raise your metabolism by the constant eating which in turn requires more energy and burns more calories.

Free day

An easy way I have found people to stick to the idea of eating healthy 95% of the time was to eat to the plan six days per week

34

and on the seventh day enjoy a free day. This is the day when you eat what you want when you want, guilt free. So all week you behave knowing that on Saturday for instance you can enjoy pizza, ice-cream and anything else your heart desires. This way you are not tempted to break during the week and enjoy it so much more on your free day than you would if you were having it all of the time.

This break in the routine also serves another purpose and that is to tell your body not to go into starvation mode where it starts storing everything, even the goods foods. This happens when you cut your meals and or calories lower than in the past, your body goes into survival mode and you start gaining weight instead of losing it. So enjoy your free day, I know I do each week; it is an important part of your weight loss program.

A fantastic book to read on eating and exercise balancing is called *Body For Life* by Bill Phillips. It is written by a body builder in a basic style which is easy to understand. As a naturopath, this is the best book I have found to date which shows you a system you can easily integrate into your daily life. If you follow the book you can restore that nutrition/exercise balance.

Drink Water

Water and in particular filtered water is essential to life. Your body is 70% water and the first place you dehydrate is your brain. Your body uses about 2 litres of water a day just standing still, that is not being a busy person racing around or working in air-conditioning etc. So you require a minimum of 10 glasses per day plus 3 glasses for every non water. Yes that means if you have tea, coffee or alcohol or soft drink, you need three extra waters for one non water. So three coffee's equals 9 extra glasses of water. So either up your water intake or reduce your non waters. Give it a try for a week and see how much more energised you feel. ●

For first acting relief,

try slowing down.

Lily Tomlin
Actress

THE GLYCAEMIC INDEX OF FOODS

The Glycaemic Index (GI) is a method of classifying the glycaemic (blood sugar) response to carbohydrate rich foods. This simply means how quick a carbohydrate reaches the blood stream. Foods are measured and ranked according to a measure of their Glycaemic Index. Foods with higher numbers, closer to 100 are digested more rapidly, and foods with a lower GI (lower numbers) are digested slower. We require a balance of both, you can have some higher GI foods, but they must be consumed with some, low GI foods to create a balance.

The foods we eat are composed of chemicals, which influence hormone responses, neurotransmitter activity and entire biochemistry of the body. Carbohydrates for example, represent a potential fuel source, but long before they are converted into ATP or stuffed into fat cells (after conversion into fatty acids) when over-consumed, they must go through a complex digestive process and then find their way into the blood stream to the liver and then connect with insulin.

What are Carbohydrates?

All dietary carbohydrates are not equal, as their rate of digestion and absorption varies. Remember how we used to refer to carbs as either simple or complex, well the simple sugars (high GI), other than fructose, tend to enter the bloodstream quickly, causing a

37

sharp rise in blood-sugar. This produces an elevated insulin response. Complex sugars (low GI), long-chain and fiber-rich carbohydrates enter the bloodstream more slowly. A moderate rise in blood sugar occurs, causing a moderate insulin response.

The Glycaemic Index

The glycemic index of carbohydrates was developed initially for diabetics. Knowing the effect of food on blood sugar is important for monitoring a diabetics glucose levels.

Foods that lead to a slow increase in blood glucose have a:
LOW GLYCEMIC INDEX.

Foods that induce a rapid rise in blood sugar have a:
HIGH GLYCEMIC INDEX.

The glycemic index measures the extent to which blood glucose increases after eating a 50g portion of carbohydrate. This increase is then compared to glucose, which is given the value of 100. Knowing the glycemic index of different fruits, vegetables and starchy foods is important because a rapid rise in insulin, can ruin your fat-reducing objectives, increase serum cholesterol levels, encourage the onset of fatigue, intensify joint inflammation and set you up for hyperinsulinemia. Remember when you eat your lunch of a day, you have a "healthy" salad and meat sandwich, an hour later you are ready for a "kindy nap". The bread in the sandwich is a high GI food, your insulin spikes and your body over reacts, draining you of energy and giving you the feeling that you need a little nap. The trick is to balance the meal so the over reaction does not occur.

Glycemic Index of Common Whole Foods

Breads				Vegetables		
Bagel		72		Carrots		49
Crumpet		69		Potato-	baked (ave)	85
Mixed grain bread (ave)		45			new (ave)	62
White bread (ave)		70			pontiac (ave)	56
Croissant		67		Parsnip		97
Fruit Loaf (white)		47		Sweet Potato		54
Rye bread		50		Peas		48
Wholemeal (ave)		77		Sweet corn		55
Breakfast Cereals				Legumes		
Kellogs All Bran		30		Baked beans (ave)		48
Kellogs Cornflakes		77		Butter beans (ave)		31
Kellogs Sustain		68		Kidney beans (ave)		27
Muesli - Toasted		56		Broad beanss (ave)		79
Kellogs Nutigrain		66		Chick peas (ave)		33
Sanitarium Weet-Bix		75		Soya beans (ave)		18
Kellogs Mini-Wheats		58				
Porridge		42		Fruit		
				Banana (ave)		53
Grains/Pasta				Grapefruit		25
Buckwheat		54		Mango		55
Rice -	Calrose	83		Cherries		22
	Basmati	58		Grapes		43
	Brown	76		Orange (ave)		43
Noodles -	instant	47				
Pasta -	Egg fettuccine	32		Snacks		
	Ravioli (meat)	39		Corn chips		72
	Spaghetti (ave)	41		Popcorn		55
				Peantus		14
Biscuits/ Cakes				Potato crisps		54
Puffed Crispbread		81				
Water Cracker		78		Diary foods		
Shredded wheatmeal		62		Milk -	whole (ave)	27
Apple muffin		44			skim	32
Ryvita		69		Yoghurt (flav, low fat)		33
Arrowroot		69		Ice cream (ave)		61
Shortbread		64				
Sponge cake		46				

You can reduce the glycemic response of a food by combining it with an essential fat or a high quality protein, both of which have low glycemic indexes. It is interesting that whole grapefruits have a glycemic index of about 25, the juice about 35.

Juicing removes most of the fiber and leaves concentrated sugars, but because grapefruit and orange juice contain mostly fructose, they still have a low glycemic effect. Eat the piece of fruit whole in preference to having juice all of the time.

Ideally, each one of your six meals per day should consist of a balance of protein, fats and carbohydrates. Remember to balance out the "carb" content of the meal so that it does not contain all high glycaemic carbs.

GARLIC- LIFE'S ESSENTIAL FOOD

Folklore and ancient history surround the humble garlic bulb, giving it a reputation that extends from warding off vampires to giving us very fragrant breath. Garlic also has a great reputation when it comes to improving our health. For centuries, garlic has been used as a virtual cure-all. Many ancient civilizations used garlic: Egyptian pharaohs were buried with carvings of garlic and onions in their tombs, while Pliny the Elder, a famous Roman naturalist, recommended garlic for everything from gastrointestinal disorders to madness! Hippocrates, the founder of modern medicine, also recommended garlic as a laxative, diuretic and in the treatment of certain tumours.

Modern science has proved that the ancient scholars were definitely on the right track. Research over the past two decades has shown that garlic may have the following healthy effects: Some evidence suggests that garlic can help prevent heart disease, heart attack and stroke by helping the blood flow, reducing cholesterol and contributing to the prevention of blood clots. Garlic has antibacterial, anti-fungal and anti-viral properties that can help the immune system. It acts as an antioxidant, fighting free radicals in the body; this can help to protect the body against pollution and toxic substances. Garlic has been shown to reduce secretions of stress hormones in experiments with mice, indicating that garlic may help to reduce stress levels..

Other than all of that, what is so special about garlic? Garlic contains about 200 compounds, including many vitamins and minerals. One of the powerful chemicals in garlic is sulphur – the chemical responsible for garlic's well-known odour. Another compound found in garlic, called alliin, it is tasteless and odourless. When the garlic is cut, the alliin converts to allicin, which has a pungent aroma, and flavour and is thought to be responsible for many of the health-giving properties of the bulb. So, once you cut, dice, chop or mince garlic, you release many of its active properties. Cooking garlic destroys these properties, so if you want to use garlic for its health benefits, raw garlic is the one to go for. I am not keen on garlic supplements as many of them are odourless and are missing this vital constituent. In my clinic, I ask my patients to peel a clove of garlic (one about the size of a capsule) and swallow it whole. It is easy to take and taken this way, it does not seem to give you the interesting aroma the next day. If you are going to take a garlic supplement, make sure to look out for one that contains allicin.

How much do you need?

The recommended dose of garlic is one to three cloves per day. If eating raw cloves proves to be difficult though, try swallowing it whole like a capsule or try a few of the followings ways:

➡ Make garlic oil by peeling and mincing 250 g fresh garlic. Place in a jar and cover with olive oil, closing the lid tightly. Allow it to stand for three or more days, shaking the jar every day. Strain the liquid, add a teaspoon of wheatgerm oil to preserve it and store it in a dark bottle in a cool place. Take half a teaspoon, three times a day or drizzle the oil on salads or other raw foods.

➡ Create a cold garlic extract by peeling and chopping five or six cloves of garlic and placing in half a cup of water. Leave for ten hours and then take three teaspoons daily.

What about fragrant breath?

If you have a meal that is loaded with garlic and want to avoid fragrant breath afterwards or the following day, chew some fresh herbs such as parsley, mint, basil or thyme. Some people may experience a body odour after eating garlic, this can usually be covered with perfume or deodorant. Personally I would rather be fragrant and healthy than not and unhealthy.

Garlic overload

Like everything in life, moderation is the key. Anaemia and inflammation of the digestive tract are two symptoms of excessive garlic intake. Excess garlic may also produce flatulence as it stirs up toxins.

Things to look out for

Raw garlic or supplements should not be taken if you are taking Warfarin as it may affect blood clotting. Garlic and other herbs, such as gingko, ginseng and St. John's wort, may prolong bleeding after surgery. Stopping the use of herbs is recommended prior to surgery, but absolutely use it in the lead up to boost the bodies healing powers.

Will it cure the common cold?

Many supplements designed specifically to treat colds and flu include garlic in their ingredients. Garlic has antibacterial, anti-fungal and anti-viral properties that may be useful in fighting colds and flu. In one study, a daily dose of 600 mg of powdered garlic was given to elderly people over a three-month time span, greatly improving their immune system as a result. So, while taking garlic may not cure you of your cold, it well improve your body's chances of fighting off any bugs it comes in contact with.

On a lighter note here are a few good reasons to eat garlic:

⇨ Bolivian bullfighters say that the smell intimidates the bull.

⇨ Soldiers in ancient Rome would chew a whole clove before they went into battle, convinced that it would give them courage.

⇨ Italian singers say that it improves the voice.

⇨ In the Middle Ages it was thought to be a cure for whooping cough.

⇨ Crushed, mixed with goose grease and rubbed into the soles of the feet, it was thought to be a cure for a sore throat.

⇨ A professor from West Germany says it clears the fatty build-up in the blood vessels and so prevents heart attacks.

⇨ About 20 per cent of people think that it keeps influenza germs away.

⇨ It keeps vampires, such as Dracula, away.

DO YOU HAVE A SPARE TYRE AROUND YOUR WAIST?

A recent meeting held by the American College of Cardiology has found that **you are what you eat** – literally. According to researchers from the Johns Hopkins Research institute, the more saturated fats you eat, such as butter and lard, the higher the level of visceral fat you have and the greater the health risk. As expected, a diet that creates less visceral fat contains more monounsaturated and polyunsaturated fats (including omega-3 fats) – present in foods such as olives, avocados, nuts, seeds, flax seeds, vegetable oils and fish oils.

Visceral fat is the fat that surrounds the organs in the abdomen. It is more metabolically active and excess amounts are associated with Metabolic Syndrome (in which high blood pressure, pre-diabetes and high blood fats occur). Visceral fat is the quickest type of fat to be laid down in the body but it is also the quickest to be burned when you begin to lose weight. Men typically have more visceral fat, the beer gut is the classic example. Where as women tend to have more subcutaneous or surface fat, cellulite is an example. This is the type of fat that accumulates more on the hips, thighs and buttocks. While subcutaneous fat is harder to shed than visceral fat, it carries less of a health risk.

A layer of subcutaneous fat over the tummy also covers the deeper visceral fat around the organs. While the relative amounts of each type of fat varies from person to person, generally, the larger the waist measurement, the more likely that the more dangerous visceral fat is present in excessive amounts. To see how you size up, check your waist measurements. The higher your waist measurement, the more risk there is that you will develop a health condition related to visceral fat. Check your measurements against this guide:

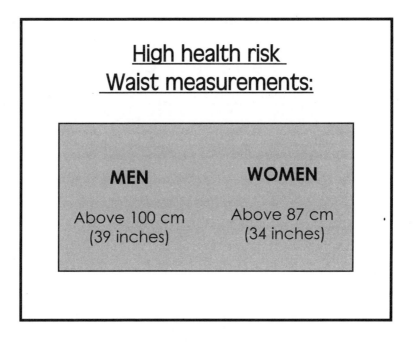

The next time you
get deeply task
orientated
take a reality check
break with friends,
family or co-workers.

Chapter 3

Live with Realistic Fitness Levels.

There are women who
sit at home and hide
their lives in unifilling jobs
because they have
believed stories that they are
too dumb,
too fat,
too old
or
too stupid
to fulfill their dreams.

We mustn't be afraid to be
ourselves and tell our stories

Kathy Bates
American Actress

I don't know about you, but I am not into the thought of having to do 10 aerobics classes a week or have to run for an hour a day to stay fit. When I was 17 I joined the regular army. As much as I loved the experience, I came to resent the endless cardio exercise program, and I vowed that I would never run again after I left the armed forces. And for the next 21 years I did not run. I would walk or look for any other style of exercise, but I would not run. Because I believed that I needed to jog for many kilometers and for long periods of time to gain real benefit.

Well thank goodness I found what I see as a wonderful balance between cardiovascular exercise and weight training. In the book *Body for Life* by Bill Phillips, Bill explains the basics of weight training in combination with good quality cardio training.

The principle difference is going for quality in your exercise training and not just quantity. As my belief in life in general is to go for quality over quantity, I gave it a go. So instead of going for a one hour jog, I now go for a 20 minute run that works as an interval training. So instead of maintaining the same pace for an hour, I jog for approx three minutes and then run flat out for one minute at a 9/10 pace. I then slow the pace back to a jog and catch my breath and build up again. I manage four intervals in a 20 minute run, eventually hitting a 10/10 on the last sprint.

Everyone can find space for a 20 minute cardio workout three times per week. It is important to go for the interval style, when you do, you will find that you are still perspiring for half an hour after the exercise. If you train in this style you will burn more calories than going for the one hour jog and it is more fun. Your body gets to the stage that it is burning calories while you are standing still.

The cardio is balanced off with weight training, again three short quality sessions. Purchasing a copy of *Body For Life* will give you all of the basic exercises you need to regain fitness. Remember it is quality not quantity. So three weight and three cardio sessions a week, which takes up less than an hour six days a week. The seventh day is one of complete rest. Like the free food day I spoke about in the last chapter, you have to have a break. If you do not rest your muscles you cannot build new muscle.

Speaking of resting muscles, your sleep or downtime is the time that you regenerate everything in your body. Aim for quality and again not quantity. Allow your body to recharge and grow new muscle.. it is the growing of new muscle that reshapes your body.

If you are a person who does lots of cardio and not weight training, you will lose weight, but unless you keep up the pace of endless cardio, or as soon as you stop, the weight goes back on. Cardio will help change size but not shape, you become a smaller shape of the original version. With weights you transform the shape of your body. The other benefit is that muscle needs more energy to keep it going, it burns more calories to maintain it, so again you are burning calories while sitting still and relaxing. You get to the stage where you do not have to continue anywhere near the level of exercise you were doing at first, and the weight stays off while you do the basics to maintain the muscle. I like the idea of working my muscles less frequently to maintain size and strength.

I meet women who say "but won't you get big and bulky like a body builder if you use weights?". It is not possible for us to build that kind of muscle. We are lacking the testosterone levels that men have to build that kind of muscle. What we will do is tone and re shape our bodies into one that is lean, shapely and strong and will help raise our confidence and self esteem.

Women know that they need lots of calcium to maintain strong bones. If you are taking calcium supplements and still not using your bones with exercise and in particular weight bearing exercise like weight training, you will still have brittle bones. You have to tell your body what to do with the calcium to gain the benefit from the supplement. So use your body or lose it.

MOTIVATION IN THE COLDER MONTHS

I spend a large part of the year speaking and conducting seminars in New Zealand. Now New Zealand is a lot colder than Queensland. To maintain my levels of fitness and health, I have to be disciplined and still do my workouts each day. I also have to be aware of not eating heavier, stodgy comfort foods in the colder weather. As the weather gets colder, it's easy to hibernate and look for the late sleep in instead of getting out and training, or curling up with a book in the evening, a heated room and friends to reinforce as to why it is too cold to go out and train. I have vivid memories of winter in Wagga Wagga; I spent three years in that town when I was in the army. Now Wagga is freezing in winter, by Queensland standards. My friends and I would spend the cold evenings eating a packet of Tim Tams and drinking two litres of Milo (made on milk). We did this night after night, comfort food at its best. Even though I was doing large amounts of physical exercise, my weight still ballooned out.

If you'd like to make it through winter without gaining weight, there are plenty of steps you can take. Here are some ideas:

Find an exercise alternative

If you normally walk, run, cycle or swim on particular days of the week, create a back up plan in case the weather is bad. Perhaps you'd like to join a gym, or invest in an exercise video that you can

54

use at home? Home exercise equipment, such as treadmills, exercise bikes, fit balls and mini-trampolines can be perfect for use inside when it's cold outside.

You may also like to think about varying your routine. If your normal exercise routine includes a lot of cardiovascular work, why not use the colder months as an opportunity to introduce strength or flexibility training into your life? A yoga or pilates class, or a session with hand weights can all be done indoors. If you enjoy swimming, many health centres have heated indoor pools where you can swim in the colder months. You could also branch out and try aqua aerobics or water walking for a change in your routine. Still aim for your intensity.

Find a friend to keep your motivation high

If you have a regular exercise date with a friend, you'll find it harder to make excuses, despite the weather. Exercising with someone else can help to keep your motivation up and make the exercise more fun by allowing you to chat as you go. Ask a friend to join you for walking, cycling, weight training, water walking, jogging, yoga, pilates or aerobics.

Experiment with new recipes

Winter doesn't necessarily have to mean stodgy comfort foods. There are plenty of delicious, warming yet healthy foods to keep you warm in the colder months. Low-fat soups and casseroles are a great option for warming you up while filling you up at the same time. Or why not experiment with some cooking styles that you may not have tried before? How about Thai or Indian dishes such as curries and spicy soups that have warm, aromatic flavours. Also keep your environment warm and you will be less tempted to eat comfort foods, invest in a good heater.

Rug up and go for a walk

Getting out for a brisk walk on a cold day can put a glow in your cheeks and a spring in your step. The cold air can be really refreshing and the break from the indoors can be a welcome relief. Be sensible, rugging up and taking an umbrella will protect you from the elements.

Take up a winter sport

For the more adventurous, how about trying a new winter sport, such as skiing or snowboarding? Or there are many team sports that are played throughout winter, such as football and hockey. Getting active outdoors can be a whole lot of fun, you can draw on the camaraderie of your team-mates to motivate you.

Don't let an old
person move
into your body.

Remember,
strong women & men
stay young.

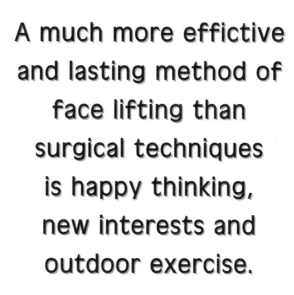

A much more effictive
and lasting method of
face lifting than
surgical techniques
is happy thinking,
new interests and
outdoor exercise.

Sara Murray Jordan

Chapter 4

Energetics of Life

Life begets life
Energy creates energy
It is by spending ones self
that one becomes Rich.

Sandra Bernhardt

WHAT FEEDS YOU ENERGY ?

FOODS: like *filtered water* feed you good energy, your body is 70% water and the first place you dehydrate is your brain. Remember your body uses about 2 litres of water a day just standing still, that is not being a busy person racing around or working in air-conditioning etc. Most people are getting around dehydrated. Water, water, water, I can't say it enough.

Brown Everything, refined grains like white bread rice and pasta leech vital minerals out of your body as well as make your body over acidic. Replace them with whole meal bread, pasta and brown rice, and you will find that you do not have that big energy drop after a meal. Watch the grain breads, as most have the grains in a white refined wheat base, making it the same as white bread.

Fruit and vegetables, common sense says that we need fresh fruit and veggies daily, ensure that you get the full range of colours with your meals. Increase the amount of dark green veggies as they are the ones full of vital minerals.

EXERCISE: Do something six days a week, whether a walk or run, an organised class, yoga or pilates, the range of exercise available is endless, just remember to include something weight bearing like some gym work and to go for quality training and not just quantity. Find yourself a style or varation of styles that you like and rotate them so that you do not get bored and give up.

POSITIVE PEOPLE AND ATTITUDES: yes we have all heard it all before, but how often do we find ourselves whining about something or someone. All it does is drain your energy. Focus on the positives in life and socialise with positive people. We all have growth cycles in life and some people get caught in negative cycles, if you have been or are in one at the moment, change your perspective to what is happening in your life. Focus on the positives and allow yourself to have a down half hour where you can feel sorry for yourself and then get on with it. Do not go draining the rest of your life and that of others because you are having a "poor me'. Life is too short to waste it. Changing your perspective is as easy as catching yourself being negative and consciously changing your thoughts.

Discontented minds and fevers of the body are not to be cured, by changing beds or businesses.

Benjamin Franklin

WHAT DRAINS YOUR ENERGY?
Get Rid of Energy Suckers

FOODS: Our bodies work the most efficiently when we work with nature, the more fresh foods free of preservatives etc the better. Have a look at what you really eat, all the things you stick into your mouth each day. What you think you eat and what you put into you mouth can be two really different things.

Some people say you cannot eat meats, it is a personal choice but if choose to do so, make sure it is good quality. Remember a small piece of good quality beef is better for you than a piece of hormone fed chicken, just remember to balance your meats with vegetables. Follow the basics, get rid of the refined sugars and grains out of your diet and replace them with living foods, plenty of fresh fruits and vegetables. Also remember it is not what you do 5% of the time, it is what you do 95% of the time that counts. We are all allowed to be human and indulge now and then.

PEOPLE: Ever noticed how someone with negative energy can suck the life out of you in a flash? Let them go, and get on with your own life and enjoy the energy that positive people feed you.

NEGATIVE HABITS: We are all human and have some negative habits and beliefs in life, do not punish yourself, reward yourself for noticing your behaviour and refocus on something positive. If you give yourself a hard time, you simply reinforce the negative and make it harder to correct the behaviour in the future. Just get on with life, it is too short for playing "poor me".

There is no scientific answer for success. You can't define it. You've simply got to live it and do it.

Anita Roddick,
founder of The Body Shop

Chapter 5

Signs & Symptoms of an Unbalanced Life

My private measure of
Success is daily.

If this were to be the
last day of my life
would I be content with it?

Jane Rule

Some of the signs & symptoms of an Unbalanced Life are:

◆   Adrenal Exhaustion

◆   Insomnia

◆   Colds, Flus & Snotty things

◆   Dull & Spotty Skin

◆   Sluggish metabolism

◆   Alzhiemer's and Parkinsons's Disease

Author of "You can heal your mind" - Frederick Bailes wrote in his book this interesting comment - its well worth thinking about -

"The body itself has no power to generate illness; illness is merely the shadow thrown by the mind. A healthy mind will shadow forth a healthy body; an unhealthy mind will shadow forth an unhealthy body. Every new cell created in the body is either negative or a positive thought in form. In the older days, it was customary to say that cells are "built under the influence" of either negative or positive thought. In reality, the cells are the thought itself. Healthy thoughts mean healthy cells; sick thoughts mean sick cells".

ADRENAL EXHAUSTION

We are born to be able to handle stress. Mother nature has given us all a set of Adrenal Glands. When you are born, your adrenals are bursting with nutrients like pantothenic acid (vitamin B5), vitamin C, potassium, zinc, and essential fatty acids. In Chinese medicine, they say that your chi lives in your kidneys. When you run out of chi (adrenal energy) you die. Your adrenals are like a bank account, every day you spend some adrenal energy, and you are meant to re-bank some energy. You are able to re-bank it by getting enough good food, good rest, and good play. The trouble is most people are in adrenal debt the majority of the time.

So what are your adrenals? The adrenals are small glands that sit on the upper inner surface of each kidney and consist of two distinct portions. The outer larger portion is called the **cortex**, and an inner portion referred to as the **medulla**.

The medulla produces adrenaline and noradrenaline, which prepares the body for how you will handle physical and emotional stress. The cortex produces cortisol and aldosterone, which are necessary to the maintenance, balance and homeostasis of the body chemistry while it is under stress. The cortex also produces sex hormones, such as those produced in the testes and ovaries. In my naturopathic clinic the primary cause I found for women experiencing menopause symptoms, was they were suffering adrenal exhaustion. This resulted in an inconsistent supply of female sex hormones and menopause symptoms.

68

Cortisol is a major player in the body's response to stress and directly influences the metabolism of sugars, proteins and fats. During a stressful event, cortisol helps maintain consistent blood sugar concentration by temporarily preventing the entrance of glucose into all tissues except the brain and the spinal cord. This forces the breakdown of muscle and other organs into amino acids, which it then helps convert into glucose for extra fuel. Without this function we would not have the fuel for the "flight or fight" response.

Consistently high cortisol levels can destroy sexual function and libido and are immunosuppressive. Stressed and anxious people, and the chronically ill, can also be increasing the rate of protein breakdown in their bodies by having cortisol levels consistently too high. This can then interfere with their recovery.

In a perfect world, we all experience an optimum state of health. If we are getting adequate good food, rest and play, the body will be strong, and illnesses and their symptoms will quickly pass and a state of wellness returned. However, if the body is continuously overworked, physically and emotionally, it learns to adapt to that repetitive stress and burnout approaches. Ever noticed at sometime in your life how you handled everything through a huge stressful period, but as soon as it all finished you fell into a heap and got really ill.

Some people stay in this coping stage for years and decades, the bodies reserves are slowly running out and they do not notice. An easy sign to look out for as to if you are running your adrenals down is: Remember how I said that in Chinese medicine your chi lives in your adrenals, well when you are depleting your chi faster than you are replacing it, "wind/cold" enters your body. "Wind/cold" are aches and they enter through that point on the crest of your shoulders. So next time you are feeling that tight and burning ache in your neck and shoulders, realise that you are running adrenaly tired.

People experience different symptoms when they are running low in adrenal energy. Symptoms like fatigue; insomnia, chronic pain, colds and flu, headaches and the accumulation of body fat with 'age' can all be part of the process. Cope with symptoms like these for long enough and our ability to handle the stress diminishes to the point where chronic disease sets in.

So what can you do for your adrenals to keep them happy and well. Relaxation techniques are a step in the right direction. Aromatherapy essential oils like Geranium and Vetiver are effective adrenal tonics. Book a regular aromatherapy massage into your diary and start using essential oils in your work and home lives to maintain some adrenal balance.

Licorice root herbal tea is also an effective adrenal tonic. You can buy it from your local health food store, it tastes like the sweet licorice, but it also has therapeutic properties. No, licorice the sweet will not substitute for the herbal tea. Two cups per day would be suitable for most people burning the candle at both ends.

Use it as a substitute for your daily coffee or tea, don't get too excited and drink too many cups in one day. Licorice root tea carries a contraindication for people experiencing high blood pressure. So if you are medicated for high blood pressure, see your naturopath before taking the tea. If you think your adrenals are approaching the exhausted stage, see a naturopath for a specific remedy for you. Otherwise don't wait to reach the exhausted stage, use the tea and oils if you are burning the candle at both ends to maintain some adrenal balance and energy. Remember a life of good food, good rest and good play will keep your adrenals happy.

INSOMNIA

As most of the population has experienced a sleepless night or two throughout their life, it is a very common complaint. Now insomnia can stem from any number of causes, worrying about work, what you did yesterday or what you are going to do today, or it could be caused from having too many stimulants during the day and into the evening like tea, coffee, alcohol or cigarettes, it could also be from eating a heavy meal late in the evening. No matter what the cause, it is a concern and needs to be addressed. Sleeplessness is classified as insomnia when it is happening repeatedly, and the whole body is suffering. You also have to consider the emotional imbalances that could be occurring.

Natural therapies and in particular aromatherapy can play a very large part in correcting a condition like insomnia. Most people are aware of using Lavender for relaxing the nervous system and assisting sleep. But there are many other useful oils. Roman Chamomile, Sweet Marjoram, Rosewood, Vetiver and Ylang Ylang are just a few others.

You have to decide what is behind your insomnia, if depression is involved, the citrus oils like Orange, Bergamot, Tangerine and Mandarin are going to lighten your spirit and assist sleeping when combined with Lavender or one of the others I mentioned. If your insomnia is caused because you are unable to switch off because you re-do everything that has happened during the day over again, you need the heavier essential oils like, Vetiver, Sandalwood and Frankincense. Blend one or more of these with Lavender and Roman Chamomile for in your oil burner or bath, and you will switch off. A simple foot massage can be enough to slow you down, if you don't have time to soak in the bath, massage your feet with a blend of essential oils like Vetiver, Lavender and Orange.

This single act could break the cycle of sleeplessness, as your feet are the fastest way to absorb essential oils in your body. Your feet are water proof but not oil proof. So there are no excuses. A 2-minute rub of the feet to get the essential oils into your body is enough to help.

Just think about this for a moment. I find it amazing that so many of us race around preparing to go out for a dinner, doing everything to make us feel good for maybe the few hours that we are out. And yet, we spend our evenings after the days work being busy, and then flop into bed and just expect to sleep, without any preparation. It is crazy but we do it.

So why not take a minute to put on an oil vapourizer when you get home so that you are letting go of some of the days worries before you get into bed. Or take the time to have a relaxing bath. The time you say that you don't have the time for it, is exactly the time you need to it. So think about it now and next time.

Nutrition can also play a very big part in preventing insomnia, foods high in Tryptophan like bananas, figs, dates, yoghurt and wholegrain crackers can help promote sleep. As tryptophan is the amino acid precursor for the neurotransmitter serotonin, which ha been found to increase sleep time.

As a general rule, it has been found that people low in calcium have trouble getting to sleep, and for those of you having trouble staying asleep, you're usually low in magnesium. Both of these are essential minerals. Also don't sit down to a large meal, too late in the evening, as it will sit heavy and still be thinking of digesting when you lay down to sleep. Your body will be using all of its energy to try and digestt eh foods and be too distracted to sleep. So, NO large meals after 8pm.

Herbal Medicine is a modality to easily integrate into your routine to help break the sleeplessness cycle. Try a cup of herbal tea. Herbs like Chamomile, Passionflowers, Hops, Catnip and Valerian root are all very useful. The only one of those that is not a real pleasant taste is the Valerian root. The others are nice and light with a little honey or lemon juice to taste. Some people have tried a tea bag version of herbal tea once and say that they do not like them now. Believe me, if you try fresh dried organic herbs you will become a convertee to herabl teas.

Common sense says to avoid consuming stimulants like caffeine, alcohol, sugar, tea, chocolate, wine, ham and soft drinks last thing at night. Try to get some exercise during the day and if possible go for a walk after the evening meal to help wear off the stresses of the day. Another thing to look out for is sleeping in a room with inadequate ventilation. As a room that is too warm or too cold can also interrupt sleep.

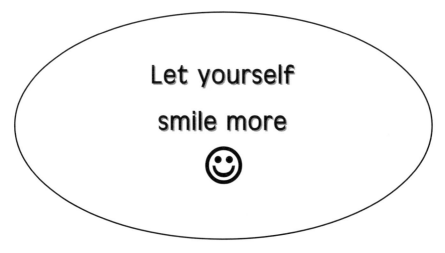

COLDS, FLU AND SNOTTY THINGS

Ever noticed that you catch a cold just when you do not have time for one. There are many elements involved in catching a cold or flu. I believe it is not just coming in contact with the bugs, but it involves how you are emotionally at the time. Have you ever said or heard anyone say how "they always catch one or two colds a year" or that if everyone else in the office has a cold, "that I will probably catch it as well." It is like they are telling their body they want it. Naturopathic philosophy says that there has to be all elements in place to "catch" something; they are attitudes and beliefs, physical stress and emotional stress. If you are not running any emotional stresses around life at the time there is a reduced chance of catching a virus etc. Take time to look at how you feel about colds and what are the stresses you are running at that moment.

Louise Hay (famous author of "You can Heal Your Life"), says that colds come when you are in overwhelm, there is too much going on and you are not giving yourself the break you need. So your body takes control and it stops you. In clinic, I have seen plenty of "snotty things" and they run with the pattern of people who are in overwhelm. Have a look at your emotional stresses and where you can rebalance life.

Australian Bush Flower remedies are excellent for addressing this side of the problem and in particular, Dagger Hakea, Paw Paw,

Jacaranda and Black-eyed Susan. They are a simple medicine you can get from your naturopath or health food store. You take the drops under your tongue and they work fantastically on the emotions behind the physical symptoms of life.

Physically, this is the time to look at nutrients such as Vitamin C. Remember don't just go for the nice tasting sugar filled vitamin C tablets. They taste great, but are not as effective as the powder drink. Vitamin C powders are marvellous and do not contain the binders and fillers needed to make a tablet.

Zinc is brilliant for immune system integrity; you can obtain it from foods like chilli and ginger, seafood's, nuts and seeds like brazil nuts and pumpkin seeds.

Most people know of Echinacea, a fantastic herb for boosting the immune system. I find that the liquid tincture is faster acting than the capsules or tablets. Although not the most pleasant taste, the benefits are worth it.

Essential oils are excellent once the symptoms are there, oils like Frankincense, Lemon, Peppermint, Thyme, Eucalyptus, Cedarwood, Cypress, and Aniseed. Oils like these in combinations are great for purifying the air, breaking up congestion and assisting your immune system. The essential oil blends are suitable for inhalations and oil burners and the ointment as a chest rub. Do not wait for the cold or flu to happen. If you start addressing these things now you can enjoy life without the discomfort.

DULL & SPOTTY SKIN
Remove toxins with Skin Brushing

Did you know you can reduce the burden on your kidneys by regular skin brushing? Sounds a bit far fetched, doesn't it? When you consider the facts, it does make sense.

The skin is the largest eliminating organ of the body. If we stimulate it in a constructive way, the skin increases its rate of elimination of toxic waste products. Less demands are then placed on the kidneys.

On each square centimeter of skin there are as many as three million cells, 15 sebaceous glands, 100 sweat glands, a metre of blood vessels, 3000 sensory cells, 4 metres of nerves, 200 pain detectors, 25 pressure sensors for touch, two cold sensors and two heat sensors.

All of these components have vital functions and brushing is the surest way of stimulating them and improving their efficiency. This type of stimulation is positive and does not lead to exhaustion, as do unnatural stimulants such as caffeine, tannins, alcohol etc.

Except when the skin is physically covered with dirt or grease, soap cannot clean it as effectively as a brush. Dry skin brushing removes the dead cells from the surface, which would eventually shed off. Because skin brushing contributes to cleansing the blood stream, it improves the skin everywhere on the body, although the skin that is brushed will benefit the most. Brushing should be carried out once or twice a day, on rising before you dress and on retiring. If you are having a shower, skin brush before the shower so that the dead skin and other debris will wash away.

Spend a few minutes brushing, working on each limb, the front of the trunk and back. Please ensure that the brush is used dry and that it is a natural vegetable fibre brush, if it is not you can damage you skin.

The really nice thing about skin brushing is that it warms the body up in less than a minute (a good thing in winter). The bottom line is that a few minutes a day will help you eliminate wastes more efficiently and improve general health and wellbeing. The vegetable fibre skin brushes are available from you local health food shop.

Try indulging in your need for "silent alone time", even if you don't know that you need it.

SLUGGISH METABOLISM

Your metabolism is the sum of all the chemical and physical changes that take place within the body to enable its continued growth and functioning. It involves the breakdown of complex organic constituents of the body with the liberation of energy, which is required for other purposes and the building up of complex substances, which form the material of the tissues and organs from simple ones. This process happens without you having to tell your body to do it. The problem is, at times in your life, the process can slow and physical imbalances can occur. The most common imbalance experienced with a slow metabolism is weight gain.

Revving up your metabolism can help you to lose weight by helping your body to burn more calories. Everyone has a different metabolism and we all have different levels of physical activity. The standard measurement for metabolism is called the Basal Metabolic Rate (BMR) and it is measured at complete rest. The BMR for women is about 1200-1400 calories per day, while for men it is 1400-1800 calories per day. Obviously, these figures will differ for each person, particularly if you have a very active job or carry out a lot of physical activity.

There are some other factors that can affect your metabolism:

Age – as we get older, we experience a decline in our BMR, normally of about two per cent for every decade over the age of 30.

Gender – men tend to have more lean muscle in their bodies than women, so their BMR is up to 15 per cent faster than women.

Weight – the heavier a person is, the higher their BMR is since they have more body mass to support.

Height – the taller a person is, the higher their BMR is since they have more body surface area (skin) exposed to the outer elements (greater heat loss).

Environmental temperature – people living in tropical or very cold climates tend to have a BMR five to 20 per cent higher than those living in temperate climates.

How to improve your metabolism

While we can't turn back the clock or change our gender or height, we can make changes to our body weight and, more importantly, our lean body mass (LBM). LBM is the mass of the essential tissues that make up our body. It includes the muscles, bones, organs (such as the liver and the heart), and the essential fat stored in the marrow of the bones and some other organs, muscles, intestines and the nervous system. The essential fat accounts for about three per cent of total body weight. In women, essential fat also includes the natural fat that accumulates on the breasts, hips and thighs – fat that is necessary for childbearing. Therefore the essential fat on a woman's body is about 12 per cent of total body weight.

So how does LBM relate to metabolism? The more muscle you have in your LBM, the higher the metabolic rate, which means that you burn more calories. Does this mean that you have to bulk up in order to increase your metabolism? The answer is no. Even slight improvements in muscle tone and build will improve your metabolism. All physical activity, including light to moderate activity, will help the tone and condition of your muscles. And a small amount of extra muscle will burn extra calories and help use fat stores.

Steps to improving your metabolic rate

Improving your metabolic rate will help you to burn more calories throughout the day. The bottom line in weight reduction is to burn more calories, this will naturally happen with the increase of lean body mass.

Here are some steps to take to improve your metabolic rate:

Step 1. If you are not exercising already, start slowly and build up the intensity and duration of your exercise sessions as you progress. Aim for 20 minutes of interval training exercise every day. Include some strength training 3-4 times per week to build or maintain muscle mass. See chapter 3

Step 2. Don't skip meals or skimp on nutrients, particularly protein. Just cutting calories will not increase your metabolism; it will slow it, as your body goes into starvation mode and start preserving everything for what it thinks is the famine ahead. Your body needs consistent levels of fuel and nutrients to keep it going. Eating a wide variety of fruits, vegetables, legumes, wholegrain foods, lean meats, eggs and dairy will provide the range of nutrients needed for a healthy metabolism. See chapter 2

Step 3. Drink plenty of water. Most of the bodies' chemical reactions take place in the medium of water, as well as their transport around the body. Eight glasses as a minimum a day are recommended. See chapter 2

Step 4. As you get older, it is more important to be aware of a balance in nutrition and to stay active. Don't use getting older to slacken off, if you stay focused through your life, the aging process is slowed and your metabolism keeps pace with you.

SAVE YOUR BRAIN
Alzheimer's and Parkinsons's Disease

In excess of 50% of all Australians who are living today will spend their latter years in nursing homes, unable to care for themselves. Scary thought, and I am sure that you do not want to be part of this statistic. The evidence is now clear that the damage found in Alzheimer's disease, is a specific part of the brain damage of usual aging, that will infect the mind of every person who fails to lead a balanced life, and protect their brain. Your brain is like any other muscle in your body, if you do not use it, you will lose it.

Parkinson's can begin at about age 35, and progresses over the next 20-30 years. You are born with approximately 400,000 nigral neurons at birth. These cells rarely divide or replicate. Your average healthy brain uses up to 20,000 nigral cells per decade after age 25. So in 50 years, by age 75, you have used up to 100,000 nigral cells, about 25% of your supply. When you get to these levels you can start to experience the Parkinsons's shake. Parkinsons's can appear before we die depending on the rate that we lose nigral cells. Environmental stressors, such as pesticides and inorganic chemicals, show rapid nigral cell loss, and increase the risk of Parkinson's dramatically. People exposed to environmental stressors begin to show Parkinson's symptoms by age 40-45.

Another major cause of damage to the brain is nitric oxide. An excess of nitric oxide readily damages the brain. It can occur with air pollution, smoking and second-hand smoke, even head trauma, physical like banging your head against a wall or negative emotions like anger and "road rage".

Short-term memory loss, loss of balance and loss of reaction speed can start showing and be measured by age 25. Your brain only weighs 2% of your body weight, but it uses 20% of your oxygen. Ten times more free radicals (nasties), are generated in your brain than elsewhere in the body. As we age this cycle of damage increases. Free radicals also damage your DNA. The hydrogen bond, which holds your DNA together, is like a zip. This weak hydrogen bond allows the double helix of your DNA to "unzip" so RNA can replicate the DNA pattern to replace any of the 100,000 different proteins required to make up your structure. The key is protein; half the dry weight of your body is protein. It is the structure of all your muscles, bones and organs, your blood, your eyes, your nerves and all your enzymes; even your genes are protein.

The codes that define different proteins can have patterns hundreds of bases long, like a string of pearls. If even one of the pearls is missing or transposed into the wrong position on the string, the pattern is distorted, the protein made from it is defective, and your life is compromised. Brain cells are mostly post-mitotic, they cannot divide and replicate themselves so they have no way of eliminating or repairing damaged DNA.

So how do you keep your brain in peak condition and minimize the risk of experiencing Alzheimer's and Parkinsons's Disease later in life? Ideally you will live a lifestyle that protects your brain from damage. Follow a balanced diet and exercise plan close to the way Mother Nature intended us to. Keep it simple, eliminating all inorganic chemicals, refined foods and energy suckers from your life. Remember to use your brain, and you will enjoy healthy brain power into your later years.

We all live our lives
with the objective
of being happy:
our lives are
all so different
and yet all
so much the same.

Anne Frank

Chapter 6

Have FUN!

If you obey
all the rules,
you miss all the fun

Katherine Hepburn

The world is too full of serious people now days. My spiritual teacher once told me that to become spiritually enlightened you simply needed to have a light spirit. And I think she was right. We get so bogged down in the happenings of day-to-day life that we forget to enjoy ourselves.

Remember how the simplest things bring a smile to your face. Well if we go back to the basics and realise the pleasure of these elements of normal daily life, we can again lighten up and enjoy the journey.

Whether you are or not into aromatherapy, get some Sweet Orange essential oil. Sweet Orange gets rid of the seriousness in adults. Whenever I think of this oil I think of Mrs Brady from the childhood television show we all know as The Brady Bunch. Remember how the worst crisis would be hitting the family, and good old Mrs Brady still got around with a big silly grin on her face and never let the troubles get to her. I know life is not always like the Brady Bunch, but maybe the secret to life is that simple. Lighten up and see what happens for you.

LAUGH YOUR WAY TO NORMAL BLOOD SUGAR LEVELS

People with Type 2 Diabetes may be better able to process sugar from meals if they laugh, according to a small study.

Researchers found that diabetics who watched a comedy show, had a similar rise in post meal blood sugar than when they listened to a non humerous lecture. The effect occured in people without diabetes as well.

Stress is known to raise the risk of elevated blood sugar, and poorly controlled blood sugar can then increase the risk of diabietes complications such as heart disease, kidney failure and blindness.

Past studies have found that positive emotions such as laughter may lower blood pressure, release endorphins, improve circulation, stimulate the nervous system, heighten the immune system and strengthen the heart.

In current studies researchers measured the blood glucose levels of 19 diabetics and five non-diabetics before and after they ate the same meal, on two seperate days. On one of the days, participants listened to a 40 minute "monotonous" lecture, while the other day they sat in the audience of a Japanese comedy show. Most participants reported that they had laughed considerably during the comedy show. In both the diabetics and non-diabetics, post meal blood glucose levels were higher after the lecture than after the comdey show.

Researchers are not certain why laughter appears to reduce blood sugar levels, but suggested that it might increase the consumptoin of energy by using abdominal muscles, or might affect the neuroendocrine system, which controls glucose levels in the blood.

Be aware of the influence of what you are doing at meal times. So many people sit down to eat the evening meal with the nightly news on in the background. It is rare that the news has a positive light hearted note to it. If you are eating and watching the negativity of the news at the same time, you literally swallow that negativity as well. So if you do need to have something going on around meal times, make it light hearted and humerous. What a wonderful way to help prevent diabetes.

LAUGHING YOUR WAY TO WELLNESS

In the book *"Anatomy of an Illness"*, Norman Cousins tells the story of how he "laughed" his way out of a crippling disease that doctors believed to be irreversible. The story goes, in August of 1964, Norman Cousins contracted a serious collagen disease, - ankylosing spondylitis. The connective tissue in his spine was disintegrating. He was told he had a one in five hundred chance of beating it, although there were no records of anyone beating the disease. Cousins was also told that adrenal stress could have been the cause behind the disease.

Norman remembered reading a book ten years earlier called *"The Stress of Life"* and how negative stress could cause adrenal exhaustion and manifest physical ailments. He wondered if negative emotions could cause disease, what could positive emotions do. Was it possible that love, hope, faith, laughter and confidence and the will to live could have a therapeutic value.

Norman Cousins planned to move out of the hospital and commenced a program *"calling for the full exercise of the affirmative emotions as a factor in enhancing body chemistry"*. He started with old re-runs of Candid Camera and Marx Brothers movies, pulled down the blinds and concentrated on enjoying himself. It worked, firstly he found that 10 minuites of genuine belly laughter had an anesthetic effect and would give him two hours of pain free sleep, without medication. Norman Cousins was eventually declared cured and went on to write his story. Seek out his book *"Anatomy of Illness"* for an inspirational read.

I was sent the following as an forwarded email that I would usually delete. But I loved it, so simple but to the point. I have no idea of the author, just one of those things that goes around the internet. So thank you to the creator of this wonderful message. Just think about it.

I'll Be Happy When.......

There is no better time than right now to be happy. Happiness is a journey, not a destination. So work like you don't need money, love like you've never been hurt, and dance like no one is watching.

We convince ourselves that life will be better after we get married, have a baby, then another. Then we ae frustrated that the kids aren't old enough and we'll be more content when they are. After that, we're frustrated that we have teenagers to deal with. We will certainly be happy when they are out of that stage. We tell ourselves that our life willbe complete when our spouse gets his or her act together, when we get a nicer car, when we are able to go on a nice vacation or when we retire.

If not now, when? Your life will always be filled with challenges. Waiting for the right time to come to be happy is useless, because the right time never comes and stuff is constantly going to keep getting in the way.

It's best to admit this to yourself and decide to be happy anyway.

So, stop waiting ...
Until your car or home are paid off.
Until you get your new car
Until you get a new home.
Until your kids leave home.
Until you go back to school.
Until you finish school.
Until you lose 10 kilograms.
Until you det married or divorced.
Until you have kids.
Until you retire.
Until Summer.
Until Autumn.
Until Winter.
Until Spring.
Until you die.
Or some other lame excuse.

Happiness is the way. So, treasure every moment that you have and treasure it more because you shared it with someone special, special enough to spend your time with. Remember that time waits for no one.

"I realise that humour
isn't for everyone.
It's only for people,
who want to have fun,
enjoy life,
and feel alive."

Anne Wilson Schaef

Chapter 7

Maintain one Calender

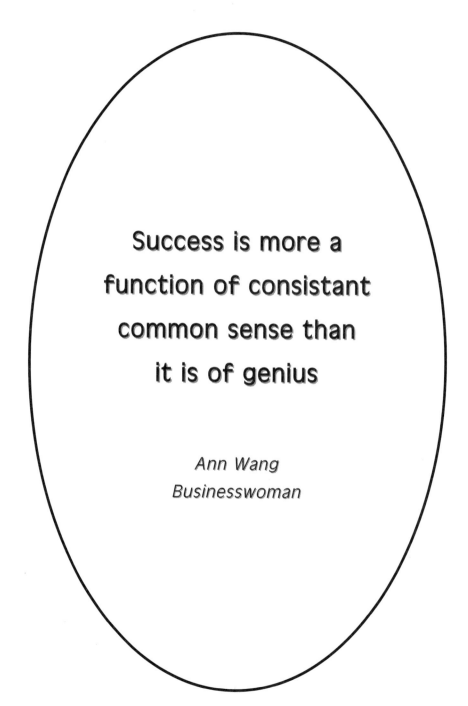

Success is more a
function of consistant
common sense than
it is of genius

Ann Wang
Businesswoman

If you are not used to having enough playtime in your life, when you start planning to change it, your old habits of letting work and other things become priority, may try to take over. The important thing is to be conscious of it and as you start to slide off track, simply guide yourself back on. You will eventually break the cycle.

If you get in the habit of scheduling everything and running one diary you will be fine. I have found endless numbers of professionals that run two diaries. A work one and a social or play one. I know when I used to do the same; I found that the work diary was always first priority. When you run one diary it is easier to maintain balance and set realistic priorities. And remember to schedule in everything, including visits to the gym for your exercise and those daily nurturing sessions or monthly massages to stay well. And if you have to go that far, schedule playtime in with your partner and kids. The same as you have systems at work, simply create a diary system to rectify something that is out of balance. You deserve playtime and your daily performance will improve once you regain some balance and increase the quality of play time. Remember we are shooting for quality and not just quantity.

SCHEDULE IN 1 HOUR TO YOURSELF <u>DAILY</u>

🕐 **10 Minutes** per day to meditate and or still your mind. Sometimes I like to rise early and watch sunrise, otherwise I will meditate. Remember meditating is just allowing your mind to be absorbed in just one thing. Be grateful and give thanks for what you do have in your life.

🕐 **10 Minutes** to be mindless, this is the time for the trashy magazine or just doing something off the planet, to give your mind a rest.

🕐 **10 Minutes** per day to read and educate yourself. This is time to yourself to catch up on some positive reading, maybe a self help book to inspire you.

🕐 **15 Minutes** per day to play with yourself. Give yourself 15 minutes to do what ever you really want to do. Free of demands of others and your own guilt. You deserve a slice of each day to yourself, no matter what size.

🕐 **15 Minutes** per day to play with someone you care about. This is 15 minutes of quality time with your partner of family or friend, a heart to heart connection. This is the time when you really be there for them and yourself. Make more heart connections in your life.

NURTURE YOURSELF

Vaporise Aromatherapy Essential Oils

When you work all day, you want to be able to just get home and relax, but many times you have family demands that can drain you. Aromatherapy is an easy modality to integrate into your environment to help you wind down faster. Now where I live if three cars are ahead of you at the traffic lights, that is peak hour traffic. Obviously some cities are worse than others for things that can drain you. The fact is that you can have a car diffuser set up to vaporise essential oils to help you wind down faster so that when you actually get home, you are home and more relaxed. This little gadget works by inserting it into your cigarette lighter and simply placing a couple of drops of essential oils on the felt pads provided. It's pretty nifty.

If you are not utilising a car diffuser you can have a vaporiser at work or at home to set an atmosphere where you can relax and handle life. Do not wait to get worked up, it takes a few seconds to put on an electric vaporiser or the car version to start making better quality down time, because you do not always have the quantity.

Aromatherapy Massage / Facials & relaxing Pamperings

Put appointments in your diary to nurture yourself. You know how you hear about the plumber who has the leaky pipes and the electrician, the faulty lights. Well the same used to be for myself, years ago as a Massage therapist I would give treatments all the time and forget to look after myself. When I finally started to burn out I realised what I was doing. So now days, I have a treatment of some description per week. The appointment goes in **my diary** and does not get changed for anything. My support team and I know the importance of my treatments and they are a priority to my well being. Have a look at where in your list of priorities your nurturing is, and if it is not high enough up the list, MOVE IT.

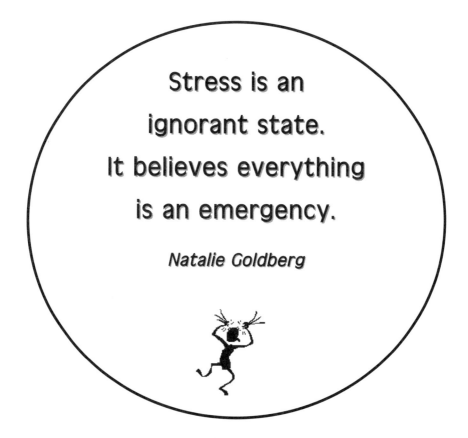

Stress is an ignorant state. It believes everything is an emergency.

Natalie Goldberg

Chapter 8

Life Balancing with Aromatherapy

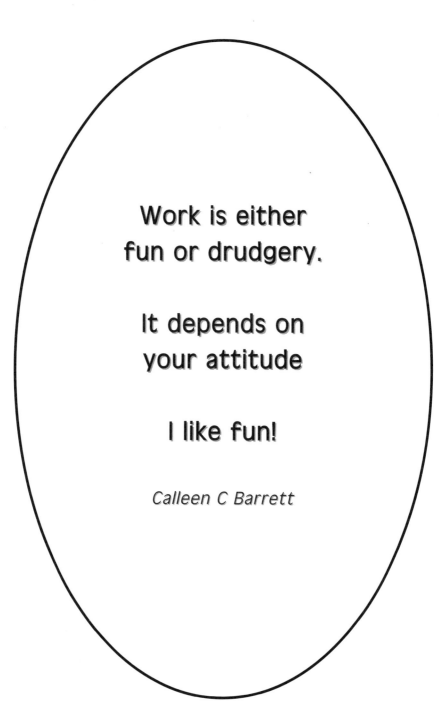

Work is either
fun or drudgery.

It depends on
your attitude

I like fun!

Calleen C Barrett

WHAT IS AROMATHERAPY?

F irstly, it is important to realise that Aromatherapy is not a *'wave the magic wand,'* quick fix for the problems and challenges of life. It is a science in the use of essential oils. This modality has seen a dramatic increase in popularity over recent years, since we all relate well to our sense of smell. Aromatherapy is a modality of natural therapy that is seriously pleasant and easy to integrate into your life. Provided you follow the basic rules outlined in this book, you should not run into trouble. It is important to consult a qualified practitioner if you have questions. A qualified practitioner of Aromatherapy will be registered with the following professional association:

The International Federation of Aromatherapists (IFA)

Aromatherapy, like all natural therapies, is very effective as a tool in preventative health care. In clinic I always had a few clients who said they have tried everything else, but nothing worked, and so they are now trying something natural. That's okay, because they now have a chance to rectify their imbalances. In Naturopathy, we talk of a person's context, that is, how everything happening within their external environment influences their internal environment, and vice versa.

If you are going to feed your body foods of low nutritional value and overwork it - abusing in it any way - you can expect a low grade of health in return.

With all areas of natural therapies, we prefer to work in the preventative field. Why wait to get ill? Natural therapies, in particular, Aromatherapy, is very easy to integrate into your work and home life. In this way you have less chance of getting ill in the first place, because you are keeping your life more balanced.

Most of the information published and the work that practitioners carry out in clinics, focuses on the physiological effects of the essential oils. In my clinic over the years, I have utilised this aspect as well. Because people are still in many instances, looking to relieve physical symptoms quickly. The essential oils are very effective at relieving the symptoms of most ailments., but what we want to do is address the cause of the imbalance.

Essential oils have many talents, their most obvious use and most frequently cited being the physiological, where the essential oils are used to treat ailments like headaches, etc. Yet the physical healing qualities are such a small part of the oils' potential. The emotional or subtle side is less well known, yet it can be the side that gives the greatest benefits because the oils also treat the *emotional* causes behind the *physical* ailments.

So what are Essessential oils?

In basic terms, the essential oils are fragrant elements that can be taken from just about any part of a plant. Like the flowers, flowering tops, leaves, fruit rinds, seeds, bark, roots, resin and berries. And in some cases several different oils can be taken from one plant. The orange tree, for example, gives Neroli from the flowers, Petitgrain from the leaves and Orange from the fruit. Each of these three essential oils has its own distinctive personality and therapeutic properties. The cost of the individual essential oils relates to how difficult the oil is to extract, and to the quantity of plant material required to manufacture the oil.

Essential oils are highly volatile, so they evaporate quickly once exposed to the air outside the bottle. They are complex chemical mixtures of organic molecules, which are safe provided they are used with care and according to their instructions.

We all have different ideas of what smells attractive. A scent that I adore could be unpleasant to another person. Your memories are linked to sense of smell, and when teaching I use the example that Lavender can be the most relaxing oil in the world. However, if a sinister person from your past, for instance, had worn the oil constantly that memory would arise whenever you smelled the oil. You would be unlikely to receive all of the relaxing benefits of the Lavender, and would probably be more on edge than relaxed. So go with scents that you personally find appealing. We are all individuals and the same scent can vary in effects between people, depending on individual chemical make-up. So again, what smells pleasant to me may not to someone else.

The essential oils are absorbed into the limbic system of the brain through the olfactory bulb and cilia in the top of the nose. While the scent is around you, your nose can become saturated with the scent. When this happens, you get to the stage where you cannot consciously smell the scent. It is like when you apply your perfume or cologne in the morning and, after half an hour, you cannot smell it any more. So you put on some more and keep doing so until you have a six-feet wide perfume cloud around you! But although you are not aware of the aroma, it is still having an influence on you. When you use your oil burner, for instance, after a while you will not consciously smell the scent unless you leave the room and then re-enter. Remember, the oil is still working. This also applies to any person who has lost, or who was born without, a sense of smell. Such people will not get to enjoy the aromas, but they will still absorb the essential oils and receive the benefits.

AROMATHERAPY SAFETY

In aromatherapy, there have been some wild claims as to the safety of the essential oils over the years. In my two previous books I also mentioned to be particularly careful with some essential oils in pregnancy for instance. With the latest research available essential oils should be considered safe during pregnancy provided that the directions for use are followed. The main one to watch is being that you do not ingest essential oils. Research has shown that essential oils are safe if they are used in the traditional ways of aromatherapy. That is through inhalation, massage and compresses. If you are in doubt check with your local qualified professional aromatherapist. The following are some safety points to remember:

☒   Do not apply pure essential oil directly onto the skin, or take internally, unless advised by a qualified and registered Aromatherapy practitioner.

☒   Never exceed the recommended dosage. Using more does not increase the oils effectiveness.

☒   Do not use exactly the same oil all of the time, as you can build up a resistance to the oil and find it not as effective. If you use synergistic blends of the oils, you will find them more effective. A synergy is a blend of three or more essential oils in the same mix that complement each other and address the disorder you want to treat.

[X]   Photosensitation: This refers to the application of essential oils onto the skin, before exposure to the sun. Vaporisation of these oils does not have the same effect. Please don't apply these oils to your skin before going in the sun, as they will make your skin burn (and not just a little bit) Bergamot, Lemon, Lime.

Aromatherapy Dilutions

Working with children calls for a lower dosage. For adults, use a 3 per cent dilution, which is about 60 drops of essential oil to 100ml of carrier oil. And for children and people with sensitive skin, use 20 drops of essential oil per 100 ml. Those drops are in total. So if you have three different essential oils in the blend, you do not add 60 drops of each for an adult strength massage oil. It would be 60 drops in total.

HOW TO USE ESSSENTIAL OILS

OIL BURNERS

I prefer to use electric oil burners. They are safe, efficient and you do not have the worry of naked flames and water. I prefer the *Aromamatic* electric oil burners. They are safe and free of mess and worry. In the morning or in preparation for a meeting etc, select the essential oils of your choice and add a total of 10 drops into the burner. Plug in the burner and turn it on. There is no need to use water and candles. The recommended electric oil burners carry the C-Tick indicating that they do not cause interference with nearby communication and electrical equipment. The ceramic bowl produces just enough heat to release the scent of the essential oil.

If you prefer the romance of the candle in the traditional oil burners, place a little water in the top of the bowl above the candle. Add 5-10 drops of essential oil onto the water and light the candle.

Remember, never leave a burning object unattended, and never leave the water in the burner to burn dry. Candle oil burners are safe to use, but do not leave them unattended. To prevent any risks and worry, use an electric oil burner like the *Aromamatic*. Both the electric and candle burners can be cleaned easily by wiping the bowl with a damp towel once you have finished with the burner.

INHALATIONS

Just like the traditional childhood steam treatment, add 5-10 drops of essential oil to a bowl of steaming water. Then place a towel over your head and bowl and inhale the vapours for a few minutes. Or, add 3-4 drops of essential oil onto a handkerchief, and hold this near the nose for a few minutes and inhale the vapours.

BODY SPRAYS

For those times when you cannot or do not want to use a burner around the office, at home or in the car, a body spray can be easily made by placing 50 drops of essential oil with 50 drops of essential oil solubiliser or vodka into 100ml of water. That is, 50 drops of essential oil in total, not 50 drops of each oil, if you are blending a few essential oils together. Add a little at a time, shake well, mist over your face or body and enjoy.

ROOM FRESHENERS

Start with a spray bottle, 100ml of filtered water, some essential oil solubiliser, or vodka, and the essential oils you are going to use. The blending is quick and easy, and you still get the benefits.

My favourite recipe for a harmonious, enthusiastic environment room freshener is as follows: This makes up 100ml of spray.

```
20 drops Bergamot
20 drops Grapefruit
10 drops Nutmeg
10 drops Pine
```

There are about 20 drops of essential oil to 1ml, so it is easy to work out dilutions. Never exceed a 3 per cent dilution in a spray, as a stronger dilution will not necessarily bring better results.

IN THE CAR

A car diffuser is available which plugs into your cigarette lighter in the car, this unit vaporises essential oils. You can also scent a tissue with a few drops of essential oil and place into the air-conditioner or heating ducts to release the scent. Scent cotton wool balls and place them in the ashtray or under the seat of the car. You can also purchase decorative, small, wooden blocks that absorb the essential oils and release them slowly. The scent lasts for a day or days, depending on the method and the oil used, and you receive the emotional and physical therapeutic properties of the particular essential oils.

MASSAGE

Massage is considered one of the oldest and simplest of all medical treatments. It is an easy process to integrate into your life, and it can procure and maintain good health. You will gain the benefits of the essential oils simply by rubbing them, diluted, onto your skin. They will be absorbed dermally and you will also receive the benefits via inhalation.

To blend a massage oil. Use between a one and three per cent dilution of the appropriate essential oil, to the carrier oil. The carrier oils recommended are cold-pressed vegetable oil base, like almond or apricot kernel. On adults, use a 3 per cent dilution, which is about 60 drops of essential oil to 100ml of carrier oil. And for children and people with sensitive skin, use 20 drops of essential oil per 100 ml.

NB: Never use mineral-based oils, such as baby oil, as carrier oils in Aromatherapy. They do not carry essential oils effectively and can cause sensitivity problems for many individuals.

BATHS

Baths are a delicious way to enjoy the benefits of Aromatherapy, receiving the benefits by absorbing them through the olfactory system (your nose) and your skin. It is like sitting in a wonderful inhalation. Breath in, and enjoy the benefits. The essential oils first need to be diluted into a base oil. You can use a normal carrier oil, but this floats on top of the water and makes a mess in the bath. If you use a dispersing bath oil base, which is a water-soluble base, there is no mess and you absorb the essential oil more efficiently. The blending is as for the massage oils. On adults, use a 3 per cent dilution, which is approximately 60 drops of essential oil to 100ml of carrier oil. And for children and people with sensitive skin, use 20 drops of essential oil per 100 ml. Then add about 10mls of that mixture to the bath.

FOOT BATHS

If you are not fortunate enough to have a bath, do not despair. You can still make a foot bath. No fancy implements are needed, a bucket of water will do the trick. You can blend the essential oils, as described above, and add them to the water. If you are going to go home and be mindless after work, try being mindless with your feet in a bucket of warm, relaxing, aromatic oils. This will improve the quality of your evening or relaxation time. Very few people these days have the quantity of relaxation time they used to have 10 years ago, so at least make yours good quality time. It is worth the five minutes it takes to make up a foot bath.

AS A PERFUME

The essential oils can be blended to make a perfume. It is easy, and there are two basic methods to choose from. Either blend 3 per cent of essential oils into a Jojoba base oil or into a perfume base made from pure alcohol and orris root powder.

A personalised Aromatherapy perfume or cologne can become an essential part of your life. You may be a shy person who needs to draw on extra courage sometimes and you could have your own personal blend that suits just you. Those around you will think that you simply enjoy wearing interesting perfumes. But you will know that you are receiving the emotional benefits of the fragrances as well.

SHOWER

Start or end the day with an aromatic shower. There are two basic methods. The first is to place a few drops of essential oil onto the wall of the shower, not in direct contact with the water, below the shower rose, for instance. The heat of the water picks up the essential oils and you are immersed in a giant inhalation. The essential oils used, will reflect the outcome of the shower.

The other method is to blend your essential oils in a non-detergent, non-scented gel base. Use this as a moisturising, aromatic, bath gel that not only cleans, but enhances your mood and emotions. It could be relaxing or invigorating, mentally stimulating or sensual. The choice is yours.

MISCELANEOUS USES

In the majority of cases, essential oils will not stain, but you do need to use common sense. If you are using oils like Vetiver or Patchouli that are dark-coloured, they can stain a little. But if a virtually clear oil like Lavender is used, you can easily place a couple of drops onto fabric. If I want to use an oil on the run, and I do not have a body mist made up, I will put a drop of essential oil onto my collar and breathe it in like an inhalation. The scent remains around me and I receive the benefits.

When I change the sheets on my bed, I place a few drops of a blend I have created using sensual and relaxing essential oils onto the sheets. Every time I climb into bed I am greeted by an intoxicating aroma that takes me off to where I want to go.

You can also add a few drops of essential oils to the final rinse of your wash, to give your clothes a fragrant wash. A friend of mine places a drop of Lavender onto the car seat so that her four-year old can have a relaxed journey.

The uses are only limited by your imagination. So expand your mind and play.

THE ESSENTIAL OILS

The following table outlines the most commonly used essential oils and their physiological and emotional benefits:

ESSENTIAL OIL	PHYSIOLOGICAL/EMOTIONAL BENEFITS
Basil	Memory and mental stimulant, nervous tension and exhaustion, brain and life overload. Enables Self-expression.
Bergamot	Acne, uplifting, antidepressant, nervousness, cold sores, stimulates urinary system. Increases feelings of cheerfulness.
Cinnamon	Coughs, colds, antiseptic, warming, arthritis, aches and pains, nervous tension and exhaustion. Removes emotional coldness and brings out your extrovert.
Cedarwood	Respiratory disorders, acne, astringent, antiseptic for skin, nervous tension, relaxant, grounding. Courage to make changes.
Clary Sage	Emotional stress, menstrual disorders, nervousness. Find clarity in what you are doing.
Clove	Analgesic, antiseptic, toothaches. Removes attachments.
Cypress	Dysmenorrhoea, cellulite, varicose veins, uplifting, respiratory sedative, asthma. For times of transition.
Chamomile German	Anti-inflammatory, sensitive skin, dermatitis, arthritis, nervous tension and stress, menstrual disorders, muscular pain. Let go of negative emotions.
Frankincense	Meditation, calming and grounding, antiseptic, astringent, expectorant, sedative. Protects you emotionally.

Fennel	Diuretic, expectorant relieves nausea and digestive disorders, stimulates estrogen, uplifting, tonifying, detoxifying. Assert yourself and complete tasks.
Grapefruit	Astringent, cellulite, lymphatic system and gall bladder stimulant, Fluid retention, uplifts the spirit. Increases optimism.
Geranium	Balances adrenals, moods and emotions. Dry and oily skin, nervous tension, sedative, uplifting, neuralgia. Balancing for perfectionist workaholics.
Ginger	Warming, arthritis, muscular aches and pains, aids digestive system disorders, nervous exhaustion and tension, catarrh and colds. Removes procrastination.
Jasmine	Aphrodisiac, relaxing and emotionally soothing, irritated skin, aids in childbirth. Regain your passion for life.
Juniper	Detoxifying, acne, dermatitis, cellulite, arthritis, invigorating, diuretic, amenorrhoea. Assists you make preparations for change.
Lavender	Headaches, relaxing, cuts, scratches bump and bites, burns, antidepressant, suitable for all skin types. Creates a safe space.
Lemon	Bactericidal, infectious diseases, improves concentration, detoxifying, oily skin. Removes irrational thoughts and behaviour.
Lemongrass	Stimulating and uplifting, indigestion. Expands the mind.
Lime	Stomach cramps, astringent, bronchitis, uplifting. Eases emotional stress.
Mandarin	Aids digestion, calming and refreshing, relieves fluid retention, colic. Gives a sense of happiness.
Marjoram	Insomnia, nervous tension, asthma, sedative. Removes anxiety.

May Chang	Cardiac tonic, antidepressant, invigorating but relaxing, hypertension. Stimulating and gives you an emotional kick up the bum.
Myrrh	Reduces inflammation, skin care, ulcers, uterine disorders, and youthful complexion. Inspires you.
Neroli	Anti-depressant, insomnia, mood enhancing, uplifting, sedative. Removes the "too hards", helps you make choices.
Nutmeg	Aids digestion, warming, arthritis, relaxing, sensual. Increases emotional energy.
Orange	Fun in a bottle, light-hearted, relaxing, nervousness,expels gas from the intestines. Removes seriousness
Patchouli	Nerve stimulant, seductive, warm and fuzzy, rejuvenating, dry and mature skin. Unites all areas of your life.
Palmarosa	Acne, skin care, hydrating, refreshes moods and emotions. Be adaptable.
Pine	Colds, flu, coughs, catarrh, sinus congestion, analgesic for muscular aches and pains. Increase self worth and esteem.
Petitgrain	Invigorating, increases awareness, aids digestion. Access stored information.
Peppermint	Analgesic, digestive disorders, antiseptic, respiratory system, menstrual cramps, headaches. Find your purpose in life.
Rose	Antidepressant, dry and mature skin, soothes heart emotions and relaxes, cooling and soothing on body systems. Nurture yourself.
Rosemary	Analgesic, arthritis, memory stimulant, mental fatigue, stimulant to liver and gall bladder. Tap into your creative side.

Rosewood	Acne relieves stress and anxiety, used extensively in skin care. Be receptive to all that is possible.
Sandalwood	Aphrodisiac, antidepressant, relaxant, bladder infections, sedative, dry and mature skin. Contemplation.
Tea Tree	Infections of all description, respiratory disorders, acne, cold sores, tinea. Understand what is really happening.
Thyme	Bacterial and viral infections, respiratory disorders, mental exhaustion, stimulant. Increases will power and strength.
Vetiver	Relaxing, grounding, reduces stress, used as a fixative. Grounding.
Ylang Ylang	Aphrodisiac, sedative, soothes nerves and anger, antidepressant, mood enhancer, releases anger and frustration.

We are surrounded
by smells.
Discover nature's
pure fragrances.
Elope to a tropical woods;
or let yourself be
carried off to a rose
or jasmine garden.

To find which oils work
best for you -

Simply Follow Your Nose.

Suzanne Fischer-Rizzi

Chapter 9

Aromatherapy in the Workplace

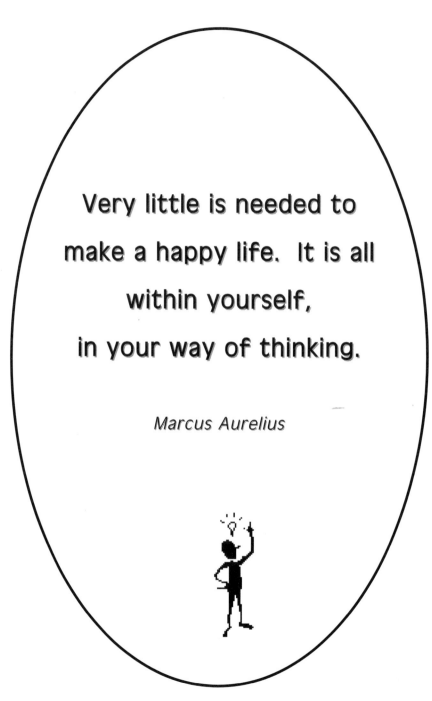

Very little is needed to make a happy life. It is all within yourself, in your way of thinking.

Marcus Aurelius

The application of essential oils into the work environment is very practical one, apart from the usual physiological benefits. Essential oils like Basil and Lemon for instance are classed as cephalics, which means to stimulate and clear the mind. In one study, lemon essential oil was found to reduce typing errors by 54%, when the essential oil was vaporised into the air. Within the workplace, essential oils can be incorporated to enhance the atmosphere for the workers, clients and the benefit of the business.

Imagine conducting meetings where the participants all band together in a positive atmosphere, allowing everyone to express their opinion and come to agreements and strategies with the minimum of fuss. The situation in the past may have been that of people not necessarily co-operating or allowing egos and emotions to get in the way. This may have meant wasted time and energy or it prevented the business implementing improvements and making change. Some people can be negative or just resistant to anything that you present, so why not utilise the talents of the essential oils to remove that resistance. Take the time to create an atmosphere where all parties are going to be more willing to engage in a positive manner. Everyone then feels comfortable and free to express their opinions, which can allow the business, the clients and the team members to grow and succeed.

Combining essential oils into a synergy of Black Pepper, Patchouli and Rosewood for instance could create an environment where the participants were feeling united and receptive, motivated and ready for change. This would be an exciting blend to infuse during a sales meeting for instance.

Or what if it was the first meeting for a new employee to meet the rest of the team. Basil, Peppermint, Lime and Cedarwood would help the new person to feel comfortable expressing themselves. Everyone would feel grounded and not threatened by the new person joining the team and you would be in a stimulating meeting environment, ready to tackle the tasks ahead.

What if you are the one going into a meeting away from your workplace, to give a presentation for instance? The chances are that they do not have an oil burner infusing essential oils into the environment like you would do, being the progressive business person that you are, why not at least prepare yourself, you could have your own, "power blend" that you mist yourself with and in the car on the way to the meeting. A blend like this could contain

Ginger,
Grapefruit,
Nutmeg
Pine.

You arrive, standing tall, energised, self-assured, and ready to take on the world optimistic and focused but in an emotional space ready to listen and negotiate.

Be in control of the work environment, set the atmosphere in advance so that the air greets all of the participants, putting them in the mood for constructive work. Progressive businesses have been utilising the essential oils for the physiological benefits like mental stimulants for years. Why not utilise the other talents as well. We are very emotional people, and when teams get together there can always be a little or a lot of tension.

For more information on aromatherapy in the workplace, consult my first book *The Scentual Way to Success* – an aromatherapy experience for business and life.

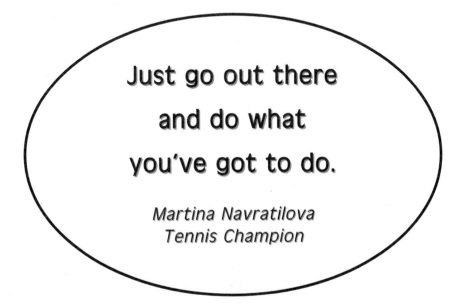

Just go out there
and do what
you've got to do.

Martina Navratilova
Tennis Champion

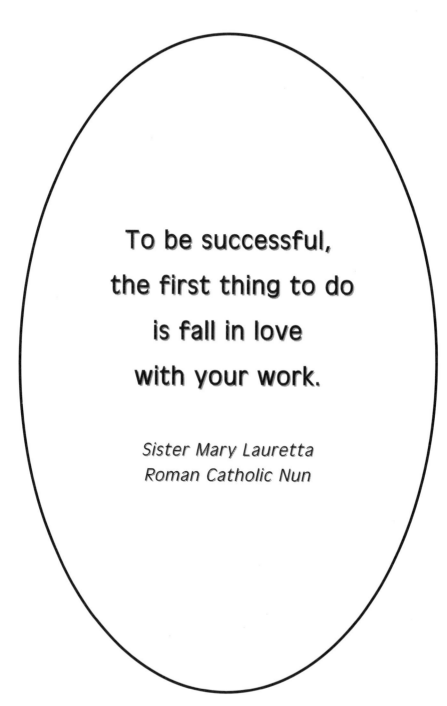

To be successful,
the first thing to do
is fall in love
with your work.

Sister Mary Lauretta
Roman Catholic Nun

Chapter 10

Live Your Dreams Now

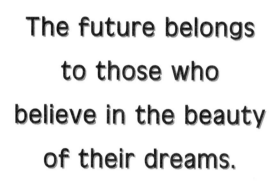

The future belongs
to those who
believe in the beauty
of their dreams.

Eleanor Roosevelt
American First Lady

DO WHAT YOU WANT TO DO, BE WHAT YOU WANT TO BE. NOW

Believe in your dreams, that is the "secret" to life. For dreams to be manifest you have to put them "out there," and start to live them now. To simplify it, how many times have you thought "I have to catch up with Mary Smith", and surprise, Mary rings you or you see Mary down the street. It is as if you put your energy and thoughts out there, and they found the person concerned. And how often have you attracted something negative by thinking things like "I don't want to see that person" or, "I don't want to catch that cold that's going around"? And, sure enough, the negative energy manifests the undesired outcome. You run into that person you are trying to avoid, or you catch the cold. So start focusing your energy on positive self-talk and affirmations. We have all heard of using affirmations: positive self talk and a positive attitude, and we have to start somewhere, so put only positives out there.

If you want a promotion at work, start *being* the person with the promotion. Don't wait. Do what you want to do and be what you want to be, now. Waiting could be fatal. We do not have a crystal ball to see everything that is around the corner, so take charge and make it happen. I recall a saying once that read:

 **Don't wait to see the light at the end of the tunnel, go down there and light it yourself'.**

Take charge now. Go and light the whole road through the tunnel, not just the end. You can be *anything* and *anyone* you want. I truly believe that.

When I look back on my life - where I came from and the path that I took to get here - I wonder how and why. I look at friends and colleagues who have not done all that they wanted to and ask "why?" Why not just do it? If there was something I wanted to do, I did it. I jumped in feet first and had a go. It did not always work out exactly as planned, but that was part of the experience I needed. You never know the who, what, when or where something is going to be a lead for you. You have to just go for it and jump in.

For 13 years I worked as a pyrotechnician (I fired off fireworks at shows), working casually for a Brisbane fireworks company. It was very much a male-dominated industry, but it was something I was interested in and wanted to do. The opportunity arose, and I went for it. I had a ball working hard and receiving the greatest buzz. I have memories that will last forever from different shows that I worked on.

Look at everything and experience as much as possible in life. Pick what works for you, and go with your beliefs and passions. Live your dreams. Do not wait for happiness to come to you, go and grab it for yourself. Of course, you may not want to be a pyrotechnician! But consider what you are doing: what is working in you life, and what is not. Stop sabotaging yourself. Make the changes and thrive on the benefits of living your dreams.

THE TOO HARD'S AND POOR ME'S

Don't let the "poor me's" or "too hard's" hold you back from living your dreams. In my clinic I have seen a lot of clients that are finding that life, and the people in it, can get a little full on sometimes. The stress, worry and frustration of this can lead to many common physical ailments, like headaches, digestive disorders and a general case of the "too hards". Everything in life just gets "too hard', dealing with people and events and people hold themselves back.

If we are not flowing "with" the changes that are happening around us, we can feel frustrated, which can lead to anger, or a range of other negative emotions and physical ailments. Aromatherapy is an easy modality to integrate into work and home to relieve some of the frustrations in life.

With the Essential Oils having their own subtle emotional talents, you can combine 3 or 4 essential oils together to make your own special blend for relieving life's frustrations. Some of the essential oils I have found to be very beneficial in these situations are:

Geranium

Known for
re-balancing
life's extremes.

Tea Tree

To help you
understand the
process occurring.

Clove

Used for removing
your attachment to
the things that are
frustrating you.

Juniper

To prepare you, and
help you prepare, for
the changes that are
happening.

If you remove your attachment to whatever it is you are holding onto (usually an expectation), you will find that the process will flow and you can act. For sure other people can be part of the equation, but you cannot really control them (even if you think you can). So just focus on your own experience and see the situation change, the frustration will subside and you can get on with your life, live your dreams and leave the other person to run the stress.

How would you use these oils? An electric burner would be the most convenient method, unless you have time to go to a clinic for an Aromatherapy Massage. Or soak in an aromatic bath at home. If you are using an electric burner , you would add 2 or 3 drops of the essential oils into the burner, switch it on and off you go. You could play with the oils to find a combination that appeals to you. We all have individual noses and as our memories are linked to aromas, it is important to have a go and design your own blend.

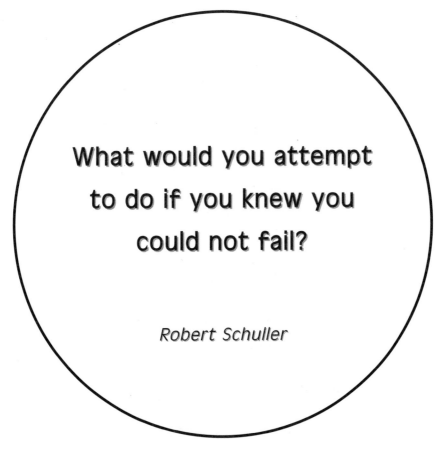

What would you attempt
to do if you knew you
could not fail?

Robert Schuller

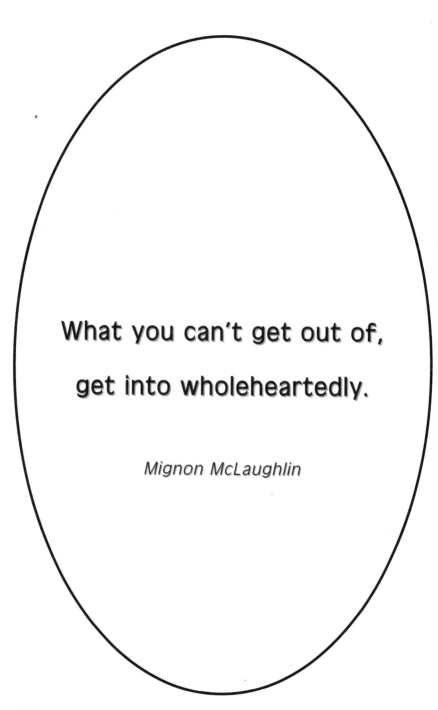

What you can't get out of,

get into wholeheartedly.

Mignon McLaughlin

Chapter 11

Remember You're Human "The World won't End"

I realised that if what
we call human nature
can be changed,
than absolutly anything
is possible.
From that moment
my life changed.

Shirley MacLaine
Actress, Dancer & Writer

The bottom line is that we are all human. No matter what you do with your life remember this, sometimes it is okay that all of the tasks are not completed in one day. The world will not end, although sometimes you may think it will. So just give yourself a break, and allow yourself to be human sometimes. The following are a couple of systems that I have learnt to live by. I have used them with many clients over the years and others have adopted them into their lives.

IF IT IS HARD TO DO,
ALL THE MORE REASON TO DO IT.

This is the rule by which I choose to live my life. If something is really hard to do or overcome - it may be a fear or just something unpleasant - we can choose to do it, to finish it, and move on. While we sustain that fear, we give away our power to it. Regain that power and just do it. Jump in feet first and stop procrastinating, then life will be more enjoyable. If it pushes your buttons a great deal, there is a special lesson to learn from doing or overcoming that obstacle. Push through and put the situation into perspective. You may have to grit your teeth or hold your breath, but when you come out the other side, you will fly. You will feel empowered, and you will know you can achieve anything.

Maybe you just need to break the problem into bite-size pieces, but at least make a start. If you keep waiting for the right time to conquer the problem - when everything is perfect - you could wait forever. So just do it, commit to yourself and your goal and make **now the right time.**

LEARN TO SPEAK FROM YOUR HEART, AND SPEAK YOUR TRUTH.

In this way you tie emotion with logic. This is not just fluffy, "hippie trippy" thinking, you will relate to all areas of your life better, and be more productive, when you are connected between reason and emotion. It is important to have your heart and head linked, although in the 1980s, many of us were not connected to anything emotional, and we now know the consequences of that folly for business.

It is strength to have your heart and head connected. Being in touch with your feelings does not make you weak, but aids you in connecting more effectively with those around you. Be the one strong enough to recognise and make positive changes in your personal and business life. Allow yourself to be human as you step outside the box, and complete the hard tasks first.

THE PAIN OF DISCIPLINE
VS
THE PAIN OF REGRET

How many times have you gone against your gut feelings and or better judgment and then kicked yourself for it? We are presented with choices every minute of every day. We decide to breathe or not. We decide to get up early or not. The list is endless and some of our choices we are comfortable with and some we are not. I always ask myself am I prepared to go through maybe some short term pain now so as to prevent the pain of regret later.

The physiological effects of emotional stress, worry, overwork and regret are far worse than those of most of the physical negatives we can do to our bodies. If you are going to over indulge in the wrong foods or beverages, take responsibility and realise that you did it to yourself, and the payoff is that you then have to have a stronger sense of self discipline to reverse any imbalance resulting from your lack of discipline. Wouldn't it be easier to have the discipline in the first place and respect yourself enough to not do emotional or physical damage to your body?

Life is simple, live it that way and you will regain that balance you have been seeking. Follow your dreams and live true to your heart. That is the secret to a balanced life.

John Harison author of "Love Your Disease"wrote in his book:

Those people who take great joy in the power they have over their own lives can fulfill their dreams. These people will become successful in what they want for themselves and will have little need for diseases. They may from time to time suffer acute complaints because of environmental hazards which combine with old childhood messages they have chosen to retain, but they will not put themselves at risk for major trauma or serious illnesses"

The Optimist's Creed

☺   Be so strong that nothing can disturb your peace of mind.

☺   Talk health, happiness and prosperity to every person you meet.

☺   Make all your friends feel there is something special in them.

☺   Look at the sunny side of everything.

☺   Think only of the best, work only for the best, and expect only the best.

☺   Be as enthusiastic about the success of others as you are about your own.

☺   Forget the mistakes of the past and press on to the greater achievements of the future.

☺   Give everyone a smile.

☺   Spend so much time improving yourself that you have no time left to criticize others.

☺   Be too big for worry and too noble for anger.

MOTIVATION

Motivation is a function of incentive born out of necessity and desire. It is fueled with a person's enthusiasm, driven by their passion, governed by positive emotion and manifested by clarity, their vision and desire for change.

So how do you stay motivated, what pushes you to get up and go each morning? What is the key that unlocks your energy, the drive and passion within you? What motivates you to be physically active, committed to a lifestyle that feeds you energy and life? Why do the majority of people not have this spark.? What has to happen to become motivated?

Do you ever wonder why someone you know, a family member or close friend just doesn't seem to care about what they are doing to their bodies and life? Is it because they don't understand the benefits of living a balanced life? I think that it is because they have not hit that point yet, that gives them the leverage on where they really are in life and what they need to do to get back on track. It is sad but most people need to hit rock bottom, getting a major disease, going financially or emotionally bankrupt or some other nasty, before they will do something about their unbalanced life.

I was the same, way out of balance for years and not noticing on where I really was in my life. For me my reality check was a car accident 14 years ago. We are all human, we allow ourselves to get caught up in the day-to-day stuff to notice what is **really** going on

142

in our lives.

Many people live in denial, not taking responsibility for what they
are doing to their physical bodies and life. How can you make
someone appreciate the advantages of living a balanced life? All
you can do is lead by example and hope that they do not get to that
place called "rock bottom" before they learn the lesson. Yes it can
take more discipline to maintain a healthy lifestyle, but I would
rather do that now while I am younger than pay for it later in life.
We all have the choice to make change, like it or not, you alone are
responsible for everything that manifestes in your life.

Personally, my rule for maintaining motivation is to live by "the
pain of discipline now versus the pain or regret" rule. I would
rather do it all now than have to "do repairs" or release regrets later
in life. Over the years I have been very human and gone off the
track at times. I find when I live by this rule, I am more inclined
to stay on track.

Now exercise and a balanced diet do require a lot of discipline at
times. You have to draw on your sense of self-discipline . Having
a sense of self-discipline will aid you more than anything else you
have in your life. Without self-discipline the mind and body
become soft. But balance is the key word here; I have seen some
people in my clinic over the years that have been unrealistically
disciplined with diet and exercise. They were off track, so
discplined trying to be good that they were doing more damage to
their bodies than good. Be realistic, listen to your body and use
self-discipline to maintain balance.

Positive Influences

Influence is a form of power, which is able to produce a result or change without any significant effort. Positive influence can produce positive changes in an individual. Influence can stir the emotions and stimulate the mind. The people you work with, play with and knock around with 'rub off' on you. Whether you recognise it or not, your associates are having an affect on your personal growth. Are your friends winning in life and pursuing excellence in their own personal development?, or do they lack motivation, direction and goals?

Have a look at who you spend your time with. High-energy people can lift you up and encourage you not to waste your life. The best kind of influence comes from optimistic people who ooze enthusiasm and show a natural talent for seeing the best in everyone. Think about who you are knocking around with, if you want to be a positive person, full of life and vigour, start including more positive people in your circle of friends.

Life Lessons

We are presented with information every moment of every dday. This builds a bank of knowledge and life experience. We know for example that physical activity and a wholesome diet are essential to the health of the human body. If you don't use it, you lose it. Loss of vitality, energy and life is the result of leading an unbalanced life. So why do so many people who have similar

144

knowledge and life skills as you, continue to ignore what seems so obvious? Because, it takes a bit of hard work and some discipline to make change in your life. In some strange way they are happier to be out of balance and be able to whinge about it than get their life together.

Knowledge is power, but only when applied. We all know people that know everything and do nothing with the knowledge. Knowledge is useless if we do not use it to improve the quality of our lives. This is evident by the fact that even people with the highest intellegence, who know exactly what to do can still have no commitment and discpline. It is clear that simply 'knowing' what must be done to be fit and healthy, disease free and living a life of passion, involves more than the knowledge alone. Nike had it right when they said, "Just do it". We have to get off our backsides and apply what we know.

State of Mind

Napoleon Hill wrote a fabulous little book called Think and Grow Rich. Throughout the novel, Hill frequently alludes to one of the most important keys for successful living: *"We become what we think about."*

If we think positive thoughts, we get positive results and likewise, if we think in negative thoughts, we get negative results. All action is preceded by thought. If we set goals and follow through with action, we will accomplish those goals. On the other hand, if we don't set goals and allow worry, fear and doubt to control our thoughts, we get what we planned for, nothing positive that will feed us energy.

We are our own worst enemy; our greatest limitations are those we create within our own mind. If we decide not to work out, eat better or get into shape, so be it. We wear the results. Negative emotions can play a powerful role in our decision making process, often they are more an expression of how we feel about ourselves and how we define our purpose in life. We all have to learn to live our own life, not get caught up in other negative peoples games. Think clearly about your goals and share them with positive people who will support and encourage you. If you know a negative person in your life that always "bags" everything that you do, don't include them in your circle. Having them negatively reinforce the experience in life, will ultimately bring you down to their level, you will not grow. And if something is not growing, then it is dying.

Professional bodybuilder Mike Mentzer describes motivation in terms of value. He explains *that value is that which we strive to gain or maintain, and that motivation, which is the inner drive that causes us to take action, is fuelled by our desire to keep or gain a certain value.*

Mentzer believes *that to stay motivated, one must learn to crush negative thought patterns by consciously choosing to focus on the positive outcome of a perceived experience. The key is to achieve mental and emotional harmony by reminding ourselves of the value of the pursuit, and to utilize both our gifts of rationality and the ability to conceptualise.*

Abraham Maslow, who wrote Motivation and Personality in 1954, he was a U.S. psychologist and philosopher. He felt that everyone functions from a 'hierarchy of needs' pattern, which ranges from basic physiological requirements to love, esteem and self-actualisation. The needs at one level must be at least partially obtained before those at the next level can function as motives to action. For example, food, shelter and safety are more important for survival than artistic desires. In societies where people struggle for life's basic necessities, scientific and contemplative habits, seldom flourish.

Maslow believed that truly healthy people seek to satisfy their highest psychological needs and were self-actualizers, fully integrating the components of their personality, or self. On the other hand, Sigmund Freud believed that inner forces and impulses, which often originate from the subconscious level, determine most of our actions.

In naturopathy we talk about a persons context. How everything that happens in the external environment of a persons body affects their inner being and how the state of their inner being reflects in their external environment. The key is to find balance internally and externally. Remove negative influences from your external environment so that there is less pressure and negative influence on your inner being.

Anthony Robbins feels that each one of us is motivated to action by our desire to gain pleasure or to avoid pain. Anthony Robbins says, *"Nothing from your past has to influence your future unless you let it"*.

So many people are letting their past actions and experiences hold them back in life now. It does not make sense; we all have the same opportunities in life. It is up to us to go out and get them.

Charles Staley suggests, *for nearly one hundred years now, our society has been living on a highly refined, processed diet. When you compare the amount of sugar and chemically altered fats we currently eat to what we did a century ago, the statistics are mind-boggling. If you can't build a healthy fit body on junk, then how can you build a healthy mind? Our gene pool has been corrupted now for over four generations...that's enough time to cause a serious amount of damage.*

Lack of motivation is an imbalance; it's not only intimately connected with our self-esteem and emotions, but it is also a function of nutritional biochemistry. Our brain, which houses our mind, is enormously sensitive to the presence or absence of nutrients in our blood. By controlling our diet and consuming balanced quantities of nutritional foods, we can definitely change our mental outlook. Motivation is the key that keeps us going when everything looks grim, when the rest give up and quit.

Behaviour therapists believe that motivation cannot exist without a goal. I believe that goals are our dreams with a time line attached.

The more strongly one feels about achieving a specific goal, the more prepared they to achieve it.

Leverage

There has to be a leverage as to why we want to follow through, like being sick of feeling and looking so unwell. The incentive to achieve, to pursue excellence and to realize our fullest potential is both a function of body and mind. To get motivated, focus on the benefits: how will you look and feel when you achieve your goal? To help me achieve my personal physical goals, I have photos of women on my bathroom mirror; they already have the bodies that I want. It helps me visualise and know what I can achieve. To stay motivated, do what works for you. Read books, listen to educational audiocassettes or CDs and watch motivational videos hang around with like-minded people. Learn to model other successful people, and don't strive for perfection, all you will do is set yourself up for failure. Perfect does not exist. Strive to improve yourself a bit more every day, be consistant, strive for progress, and achieve your own personal best.

Motivated people are happy, high-energy people. They know what they want, and they are willing to pay the price for being disciplined. Remember, personal power is the ability to take action, to set straight once and for all what it is you want to do and whom you want to be. It is overcoming the hurdles of life and disregarding the doubts and fears, driving onward and upward against all odds. The more you give it a go, the more you have the enrgy to keep going. The momentum of positive change keeps you motivated. Everyone knows that once you have been going to the gym for a few weeks it gets much easier.

Focus

Focus on looking good and feeling stronger. Focus on your goals and let the discipline of life permeate into every component of your being. Feed your mind with mental protein. As you make progress and incorporate new changes for the better, exercise, nutrition and a positiv e lifestyle will become second nature.

Remember that our state of mind is always up to us. Living life is our choice. We can't always control what happens around us, but we can control how we respond to every situation. What we feed our mind will determine the extent to which our mind can grow and develop. It's like nutrition for the body. The body loves natural food and the mind loves to be stimulated and challenged. We have control over what we feed our mind the majority of the time. We are in control. So feed your mind with the highest quality information you can find.

Persisting and being consistent in everything you do is what brings you the rewards. Stopping and starting will get you nowhere. No matter how tough things get or how busy you are, if you are discplined you can always go to the gym and channel out stress and negative energy, instead of losing control and destroying your body.

150

Personally I know how I have benefited by rebalancing my life, after I resigned from the regular army twenty-one years ago, I vowed I would never exercise again. I'd had enough of doing it because I was told to. Over the years of not doing structured exercise, my body started getting old, I was paying for my laziness. Now days I cannot wait to exercise, the buzz I feel outweighs any pain I experience for having done the exercise. Training regularly feels great and helps keep everything focused, including what and when you eat. It's like a stabilizer. Exercise will add to your self-confidence and keep your anabolic drive alive. This will give you the sensation of power and inner vitality. A strong, flexibile body that is well conditioned will provide you with a certain quality of living unattainable any other way.

Today I feel emotionally and physically fitter now than I did when I was 20years old and a soldier in the Australian regular army.

Every one of us has endless potential and value. It's been said that each of us has a genius inside, we all ahve something unique to share. It's important to believe in yourself and to recognize what your special quality is. Part of our design and makeup is dependent on using our bodies creatively in a physical fashion, in balance and with a sense of purpose.

There are many physically and emotionally challenged people out there who would love to be able to do half the things that yuo can do. So get off your lazy backside and do something with your life. Don't let an old person move into your body.

Go with life
&
Enjoy the journey

Bibliography

Bailes F. *Your Mind Can Heal You* – DeVorss & Co USA (1971)

Battaglia, S. *The Complete Guide to Aromatherapy.* The Perfect Potion, Australia, (1995).

Cousins N *Anatomy of an Illness* – W.W. Norton & Company Inc. New York (1979)

Colgan M. *All New Sports Nutrition Guide* - Apple Publishing Company Canada (2002)

Dethlefsen T. & Dahlke R. *The Healing Power of Illness* – Element Books USA (1991)

Harrison Dr J. *Love Your Disease* - P37 Harper Collins Australia (1992)

Hay L. *You Can Heal Your Life* – Specialist Publications Australia (1984)

Jefferies J. *Scentual Way to Success* – Living Energy Australia (1999)

Jefferies J. & Osborn K. *Aromatherapy Insight Cards* – Living Energy Australia (2001)

Phillips B. *Body for Life* - Harpercollins Publishers USA (1999)

Jennifer Jefferies ND. APS
Life Balancing Specialist

Jennifer Jefferies is a Life Balancing Specialist. Jennifer works as a Professional Speaker, Naturopath, and Aromatherapist. She has over 14 years experience in clinic and training, and travels Australia and Internationally speaking to business groups on Balancing Work and Play and preventing burnout in the workplace.

Jennifer has personally traveled the road to ill health and business burnout and back. From being indoctrinated into the regimented work ethic of the Regular Army at 17 to exploring new directions in personal growth and development. Jennifer has now arrived at a time in her life where she only does what she is truly passionate about.

Jennifer's passion in life is informing people on ways that they too can integrate natural therapies into their work and personal lives to achieve the feeling that they are really LIVING and not just EXISTING. Jennifer is an entertaining professional speaker who enthuses her audience to stop just existing and to really start living again.

Other Publications by the Author

The Scentual Way to Success,

"An Aromatherapy Experience for Business and Life". This is the book, for learning how to integrate aromatherapy into the workplace. Learn the subtle, yet powerful emotional benefits of aromatherapy essential oils.

THE AROMATHERAPY INSIGHT CARDS.

Everybody knows that they have let themselves go off track lately. The problem is now days is that poeple are closed to the endless posibilities of life, they cannot find a way out of the mess. This set of cards is designed to develop intuition, emotional awareness and knowledge of Aromatherapy, so that you can tap into your intuition and be guided to the answerrs you seek.

Calm Kids A guide to natural therapies for children

Kids of all sizes get wound up at times and lend themselves to the bumps and adventures of life. Natural therapies are a subtle but powerful way of aiding children's health problems and imbalances and returning that sense of good health and well-being. Learn effective treatments and how to implement aromatherapy essential oils, balanced nutrition and exercise in the home environment to create positive, supportive surroundings for the whole family. Help your children relax and sleep well, improve their appetite and immune system, watch them to concentrate with their studies, balance mood swings and hormonal changes

Recommended Suppliers and Aromatherapy Services

If you have trouble sourcing qualified practitioners or quality essential oils in your area, I can recommend the following companies for you to contact.

Australia

Aromamatic Products
www.aromamatic.com.au

Australian Bush Flower Essences
www.ausflowers.com.au

International Federation of
Aromatherapists
www.ifa.org.au

Living Energy Natural Therapies
www.livingenergy.com.au

Michelle and Shane Reinhardt
Independent LeReve Executive
Directors
www.aromacareers.com
Email : shanelles@aromacareers.com

Plant Essentials
www.plantessentials.com.au
Email : toni@plantessentials.com.au

Springfields Aromatherapy
www.springfieldsaroma.com

The Perfect Potion
www.perfectpotion.com.au

New Zealand

The Oil Well
aromanz@xtra.co.nz

United Kingdom

Fragrant Earth
www.fragrant-earth.com

Jennifer is always pleased to hear of your personal experiences with natural therapies. Feel free to write to her at **jennifer@livingenergy.com.au.** Jennifer travels Australia and Internationally and is available for workshops and seminars in your area. For information on Jennifer's other books and presentations go to **www.livingenergy.com.au**

Jennifer's Presentations Include:

Calm Kids

Learn how to integrate natural therapies into the home environment to create positive and supportive surroundings for the whole family. Help your children relax and sleep well, improve concentration with their studies and life, and balance mood swings. Help guide them into taking responsibility for their own lives and actions.

Balancing Work and Play

The majority of people nowadays have less playtime than they generally had 5 years ago. This is probably not going to change in the near future. So the secret is to learn how to have better quality of playtime when you no longer have the quantity of playtime. In this presentation you will learn the "7 Steps to Sanity" and how to integrate natural therapies into work and play to produce a more balanced and effective life.

Energetics of Aromatherapy Essential Oils

Explore the emotional and subtle side of pure aromatherapy essential oils and how they can benefit your life. Learn about The Triangle of Health and how to use, The Aromatherapy Insight Cards and pendulums to discover new ways to work with your intuition, selecting essential oils most beneficial for you to rebalance your personal and business life.

Body for Life

Imagine, just 12 weeks from now, having the lean, healthy body you've always wanted and not having to turn your life upside down to get it. Imagine having the energy to be at your peak from dawn to dusk, having confidence to do all the things you've been putting off, having the certainty to make the right decision at the right time, and knowing that you really do have the power to change – not just your body but anything in the world that you set your mind to. Go to our website www.livingenergy.com.au to see how we transformed our bodies and lives.

Detoxifying Naturally

In this educational seminar you will discover how essential oils, foods and herbs can cleanse your body and improve your health and well being.

E-Scentual Woman

Designed for women tired from running busy work and home lives, leaving themselves no time to relax and nurture themselves. Learn how to get in touch with your strength, your feminine spirit, and which natural therapies to use to re-ignite your passion for life.

Introduction to Aromatherapy

This full day workshop teaches you the basics in understanding the correct way to use essential oils, methods of application and safety. Also learn which aromatherapy remedies to use for common ailments across all body systems, and discover the creative art of blending essential oils for therapeutic purposes and blend your own massage oil to take home.

Women's Health

Aromatherapy is considered one of the most effective methods of dealing with menstrual, pregnancy and menopausal problems. Many essential oils & herbs can help to regulate hormone production, can relax or uplift, or are useful for reducing stress-related tension that often exacerbates symptoms. In this seminar you will learn which essential oils & herbs are useful for stress burnout, tired adrenals and reproductive system imbalances.

Jennifer is available for
key·note presentations,
seminars and workshops.

For further information contact

Jennifer Jefferies

Email : jennifer@livingenergy.com.au

Website : www.livingenergy.com.au